1195

W9-CXC-233

Feeling Good

About Myself

Feeling Good About Myself

By
HILEY H. WARD

THE WESTMINSTER PRESS
PHILADELPHIA

Grateful acknowledgment is made to the following for the use of excerpts
from copyrighted material:

Addison-Wesley Publishing Company, Inc., Buff Bradley, *Endings*, ©
1979; and Philip G. Zimbardo, *Shyness*, copyright © 1978.

E. P. Dutton, John Irving, *The Hotel New Hampshire*, copyright © 1981 by
Garp Enterprises, Ltd.

McGraw-Hill Book Company, Margaret Hyde, *Mind Drugs*, copyright
1974.

Julian Messner, a Simon & Schuster division of Gulf & Western Corporation, Dianna Daniels Booher, *Coping: When Your Family Falls Apart*,
copyright © 1979 by Dianna Daniels Booher.

First names used in this book are fictitious, although the material is real.
Where full names are used, permission was obtained. Statements not
attributed are from personal letters or interviews.—H.W.

First edition
Published by The Westminster Press®
Philadelphia, Pennsylvania

PRINTED IN THE UNITED STATES OF AMERICA
9 8 7 6 5 4 3 2

Library of Congress Cataloging in Publication Data

Ward, Hiley H.
  Feeling good about myself.

  Bibliography: p.
  Includes index.
  1. Adolescence—Case studies. 2. Adolescent
psychology—United States—Case studies. 3. Youth—
United States—Attitudes—Case studies. I. Title.
HQ35.W37 1983   305.2'35   82-25613
ISBN 0-664-32704-4

To my wife and helper
JOAN BASTEL

Contents

Introduction

Adolescence can be the best of times and the worst of times. Dr. Hiley Ward in FEELING GOOD ABOUT MYSELF has captured the many highs and lows that face today's teenagers. This book is like a road map that will guide you up the mountains of adolescent ecstasy and down into the valleys of adolescent despair. Yet this book is a road map of distinction: it is full of helpful guideposts that you can use to complete a safe journey into adulthood.

It is difficult to be a teenager today. Boys and girls are entering puberty much earlier than their parents did. No wonder it's so hard for parents to be very helpful when their own recollections of adolescence just don't seem to fit with today's world. One of the things I like most about this book, then, is that Dr. Ward has gone out into the real world and talked to the kids themselves: the real "experts" on what it's like to be a teenager today. The result is that this book is alive and true. I think that you will surely find yourself within these pages and your friends as well.

While I believe the book will appeal mostly to fifth-, sixth-, and seventh-graders, those youngsters who are just entering puberty and adolescence, there is a lot of information that fourteen-, fifteen-, and even sixteen-year-olds might find useful.

When I gave a twelve-year-old neighbor of mine a sneak

preview of Dr. Ward's manuscript, she replied, "Yes, this is a book for 'born again' kids."

I thought she had missed the point. "Born again? What do you mean? This isn't a book on religion," I answered.

"I know, I know," she laughed. "Born again from the life of childhood into the second life of adolescence!"

Yes, that's it. This book is about entering a new life, certainly a whole new phase of life. It is a life of new feelings, new ideas and values, new challenges and opportunities. It is about a rebirth of sorts, a rite of passage.

In the hands of the author the passage of adolescence is treated warmly, gently, and positively. Dr. Ward does not come from the "cool school" of writers who glibly advise kids to go out and do their own thing, to reinvent the wheel for themselves. He seems to know that too many teenagers, if left entirely on their own, get run over by that wheel before they even get a chance to discover it. Yet, I'm pleased to say that the author is not a rigid "heavy" either. He's not out to con you or to scare you. I think you'll find this book an honest effort both to tell you how it really is and to offer some sensible, middle-of-the road advice.

Reading this book should be fun. It's like reading a good story, except that you are the star. It's like taking a short course on the subject of adolescence, a study of yourself, the most fascinating subject of all.

One more thing. Please share this book with your parents. FEELING GOOD ABOUT MYSELF could really serve as a great springboard for spirited family discussion. Most Moms and Dads would appreciate a little education about what it's really like to be a teenager today. I know that the author would approve. He's obviously a friend of teenagers, but he also respects parents. I like that.

JOSEPH R. NOVELLO, M.D.

Washington, D.C.

ANGER/TEMPER

1

Take a Walk

Suddenly it's more than you can handle—you scream, you bang doors. It's anger. If you become madder and meaner than one might expect, it's temper. If you do it regularly, especially to get a desired result, it's a temper tantrum.

Kids in Maryann DiDomenici's class at Eisenhower Middle School in Norristown, Pennsylvania, admit there are times when they have lost their temper:

—"I lost my temper when my brother took my five dollars and spent it."—Boy, 12.

—"My cousin pushed me into a brick wall. I sat down and his game was there. I didn't look where I sat, and he pushed me off his game and into a brick wall. So I lost my temper and we got into a fight."—Girl, 12.

—"I lost my temper with my cousin because she was making a fool of herself and I told her but she got really mad and so did I. We just started arguing and then I went home because I was so mad."—Girl, 13.

—"I was walking in a field, me and my friend, and all of a sudden I got hit in the forehead with a rock. Me and my friend ran up the hill and I just lost my temper and started to freak out."—Boy, 12.

—"I really get mad when someone tries to be funny by smacking you in the arm, and when you get mad they make up dumb excuses like, 'I won't hit you if you say hi more often.' "—Boy, 13.

—"My sister tried to blackmail me and I slapped her face and busted her lip."—Boy, 12.

—"I lost my temper when I could not go some place that I wanted to go, and I lose my temper on anybody that would say anything to me."—Girl, 13.

Why do people lose their temper? Is there one thing that stands out as a reason?

Do you remember a time when you lost your temper? Why did you lose it?

Did you have to lose your temper?

Are there other ways to let off steam besides blasting off?

Some people get hurt, even killed (they call it manslaughter), by people who lose their temper.

Actually, getting mad and losing one's temper may bring more problems, according to psychologist Carol Tauris in her book *Anger: The Misunderstood Emotion* (Simon & Schuster, 1982). Instead of serving to let off steam, the venting of anger makes a person more uptight with hostility and anxiety, she says.

Losing your temper may be something you have to do, but watch out if you lash into a temper fit too often. Your temper fit might tell more about you than about the other person.

Dr. Robert Nicolay, a professor of psychology at Loyola University in Chicago, who has testified in many famous trials, says that "temper is a lot more controllable than you think."

"For example," he says, "suppose a policeman is standing next to you. Would you really lose your temper?"

Dr. Nicolay pulls no punches on temper. He says:

"First of all, you're kidding yourself if you think you can't control temper, and second, it's dumb. People don't like to be dumb. Losing your temper isn't very smart, because it means you have run out of other techniques and you are not smart enough to try another way."

Harvey A. Rosenstock, medical director of the Adolescent Center at Houston International Hospital, tells of parents and kids who use a "contra" technique—that is, they change the subject, then turn it around and reverse the situation. He recalls:

"One memorable example occurred when the mother of an adolescent boy, in the heat of an argument, suddenly turned to her son and said 'Australia.' After a brief silence, he retorted, 'New Zealand.' Then both broke into smiles. What followed was a more constructive pursuit of answers to the question 'What are we really fighting about?' " (In Leonard Gross's *The Parents' Guide to Teenagers,* p. 45; Macmillan, 1981)

Temper comes from frustration. So one way to fight it is to put a little time between you and the person or thing you are steaming about. Go for a walk, leave the scene, count to ten before responding, relax, and try to think it out. If there's something to fix, come back to it at another time.

You can always get angry later, if you feel you must. Usually time and a short wait will defuse your temper.

Said one twelve-year-old boy at Eisenhower: "You should not do too much. You should relax more often. When your mother yells at you for something, don't yell back."

Said a girl, age thirteen: "Let it all out on a plant."

BOREDOM

2

This Is Fun?

"It's rainy, and it's rained every weekend for months. I'm bored. There's nothing to do."

"Every day is the same. Up early. School. Boring classes. Long lunch line. Dull books. Homework."

"It's mid-February. Will spring ever come?"

Or: "It's midsummer. I've done it all. What else is there? Vacation? Traveling long hours can be boring."

Life can be a bore. So can people. Anything can be boring and often is.

You do not have to be serving a life sentence in a federal penitentiary to be bored. Boredom comes in both small and large doses to everybody, and there may be some of it every day.

Boredom is not so simple as it sounds. Boredom is complex. For when you are talking about boredom, you may really be talking about something else.

"Boredom is akin to laziness," says psychologist Robert Nicolay. "People who say they are bored mean 'I don't know.' " To Dr. Nicolay, the bored person may just not be very smart, at least not smart enough to figure out how to keep from being bored.

Dr. Tony Meade of the Illinois Institute for Juvenile Research in Chicago has another point of view. People who say they are bored may mean they are unhappy and not having any fun.

16

There is also a selfish side to boredom. Dr. Nicolay says that "boredom is when you don't relate to anything beyond yourself." Randy Wessel, who works with police officers in his assignment at the Illinois Institute for Juvenile Research, feels that one way to fight boredom is to invest yourself and your time with others.

What do you mean when you say you are bored?

What might you really be saying when you say you are bored?

Is there anything in life that might not become boring at some point? Could a ball game become boring, or video games, or TV, or your best friend?

Was there a time when you were bored, but found a way to escape the boredom?

What's the most boring thing in the world?

What's the most exciting thing in the world?

Being bored is like saying you've tried everything, and that nothing is going to help. How can you help a little brother or sister who insists that he or she is bored? Nothing helps!

Nothing helps unless you learn to figure out why you are bored and what you mean. Then you can deal with your feeling. If being "bored" means you are unhappy, then there are ways to be happy. And some famous scientists like Thomas Edison, have been very happy when they seemed to be bored, following the same routine and doing the same experiments over and over.

Debbie Denny of the Illinois Institute for Juvenile Research explains that all of us have to realize that life is not always fun and games.

So she suggests that we identify other experiences that are not necessarily fun but are enjoyable, look forward to them, and develop them.

For example, dinner is generally enjoyable, although not

a rip-tearing fun time. Perhaps you can become involved in the dinner preparation, she says.

Or think about the walk to school on a nice day. There are interesting lines on the sidewalk to follow, some pets along the way, stones to throw at cans in a junk lot, and so forth.

You might even try a different route to school, just to break the usual pattern. "Active interventions"—breaking routines—is one way of becoming unbored, according to Dr. Meade.

Getting rid of boredom may come down, in the long run, to being as creative as you can.

If you are bored during a long car ride, play some games. You know many car games, such as thinking of an object or a person and having those in the car guess what it is, starting with animal, vegetable, or mineral; or finding words along the highway, starting with the letters of the alphabet from *A* to *Z*. A variation on the sign game is to read signs you see in a funny way—run all the words together or mix them with other signs.

And if you have idle moments, daydream. "There's nothing wrong with daydreams," says Debbie Denny. And Tony Meade remarks that "daydreams will help you to fall asleep, if you are a little unhappy." And daydreams offer hopes, things to look forward to.

"Daydreaming is the most natural activity in the world," says Dr. Salvatore Didato, a New York psychologist.

Writing in *Kidbits* magazine (May 1981), he said: "Daydreams appear to be only idle thoughts which drift in and out of our heads like sailboats in a gentle breeze, but actually they are caused by something definite which is on our mind. It might be a wish to escape a boring class, a desire to be with a friend, or an attempt to solve something which bugs us. Daydreams are a special form of thinking, and they usually involve mental images—pictures in the mind's eye."

That leads Dr. Didato, who wrote several books, to suggest ways you can make your daydreams helpful. You can use daydreams to smooth out your worries and, at the same time, stretch your imagination, he says. "The trick is to shape and guide your daydreams into constructive thinking that will work for you."

So he comes up with what he calls "guided imagery," a game of managing the pictures in your head.

For example: "Let's say you're uptight about an upcoming party or an oral report you'll give in class. Relax your mind and let your thoughts come and go. Pretend there's a TV in your head, then picture yourself on it saying and doing things that will be helpful for you, not only things that you like most. Picture yourself as relaxed, confident and smiling.

"Later, at class or at the party, the situation will be easier for you to handle. The guided daydream is a kind of mental rehearsal, and it really does work."

3

Close Encounters
of a Warring Kind

"Sometimes he's nice to me if he wants something," says Rhonda Bastel, twelve, of Overland Park, Kansas, of her brother, Paul.

He is about three years older, and they have had happy times, and they have quarreled, typical of kids growing up in normal families.

But, as her grandmother puts it, Rhonda and Paul are lucky—they have parents they can talk to.

In troubled homes where brothers and sisters are forced closer together, they may not be so lucky.

Too much loyalty and dependence on one another may cause brothers and sisters to lose a sense of identity. It is a problem of twins growing up together—they are not treated as two persons, but as one, very much alike, since they even look alike.

Says Virginia Adams in *Psychology Today* (June 1981): "If parents thought more about it, they might worry a bit less about signs of rivalry and a bit more about excessively close ties. They might look up the story of Dorothy Wordsworth, sister of the poet, who gave her life entirely to her brother William, renouncing any independent existence of her own."

Rhonda reported that if she did something, her brother, Paul, would laugh and call her names. He'd say, "I'm boss, I'm older," and he'd say, "Just do what I want."

Sometimes he'd beat her up. Sometimes she'd threaten him or promise to tell on him.

"He'd stop when I said I'd tell on him, but then I'd tell on him anyway."

"Yes, he'd stop, or get meaner."

Besides telling on him, she had other ways of holding her own. If he were calling her names for whatever reason, she'd say, "All right, be quiet, or I leave," or, if he was mad, she'd call him names right back, and bug him, just to get back at him.

But the two knew how to be nice to each other, "especially if Mom was mad, and we didn't want to make her madder."

But brothers and sisters in rivalry can also be nice to each other, just because they want to. Rhonda admits, "Sometimes I get him a Coke, when I'm up from TV—unless, of course, I'm mad at him." Paul can be very nice, too, and he's building her a three-story dollhouse.

What do brothers and sisters fight over most?

Do you have brothers and sisters? Are your experiences different from Rhonda's?

How would you change your brother or sister if you could?

If it's not your turn to do something, but your parents tell you to do it anyway, what should you do?

How long should you stay mad at a brother or sister?

Rhonda has this advice for getting along with an older brother, and it could also work for a brother getting along with an older sister:

1. "When he's mean to you, ignore him, and be nice back."
2. "Be first to do something nice."
3. "If he puts you down, start laughing."
4. "Listen to him once in a while."

5. "If being nice and stuff like that doesn't work, and he's mad and mean, don't forget you can always tell Mom!"

Psychologists add these suggestions:

1. Treat your brother or sister as a person, not as a pet to protect or as a punching bag.
2. Roll with the punches. Remember, brother-sister rivalry is not bad. In fact, it's normal.
3. Be yourself. Respond the way you feel like responding.
4. At times, be patient, especially if you want to turn the situation around. A wait-and-see approach may defuse the time bomb and the brother or sister might stop teasing if there is no response.
5. Go ahead and compete. If you want to play the same band instrument, play the same sports, try out for the same team, have the same hobby—why not? There's no law against it. Don't be put off because a brother or sister has been there first.

There have been brother-sister successes in the same field—Eric and Beth Heiden, both holding world records in speed skating; Philip and Nancy McKeon, appearing in *Alice* and *Facts of Life* on television. And there are the two sisters, Ann Landers and Abigail Van Buren, with their advice columns in rival newspapers.

Competing may be the natural thing to do, two children following in Dad's or Mom's footsteps, as with Jane and Peter Fonda in the footsteps of actor-dad Henry Fonda; or the Boone sisters in the steps of singer-dad Pat Boone; or Aretha and Caroline Franklin, in the footsteps of their dad, preacher and singer C. L. Franklin; or Frank and Nancy Sinatra in the steps of singer-dad Frank Sinatra; or the family of Wyeths, where nearly everyone is a famous painter; and so on.

Realizing just where you are on the age scale, or where you are in the family, might help, says Dr. Joseph R. Novello, director, Child and Adolescent Services, The Psychiatric Institute, Washington, D. C. We do inherit certain roles in life, but they are always changing, he says.

And keep in mind that your relationship with big brother or sister will change. Eric K. Goodman, in *Seventeen* (March 1981), says that many girls ages eight to fourteen have the urge to choke their brothers, but can't (he's too strong). Yet this changes as high school comes along. Goodman says:

"The squabbling that kids are prone to just before and while passing through puberty—when they don't know exactly what to think of the opposite sex except that they're weird—often comes to an end when one or both siblings enter high school. Relationships then normalize. You may never be close friends, but you can again remember and appreciate his good points—like the afternoon he taught you to ride without training wheels."

CLOTHES

4

Leave the Snakes at Home

The announcement came like a thunderbolt over the loudspeaker system at Swarthmore (Pennsylvania) High. There would be a dress code.

The students were not used to being told what to wear.

And as if that were not enough, the writings of controversial people were banned. In one class, Sigmund Freud, Vienna psychologist who had written a lot about sex, was to be banned. In another class, it was an East German book that was banned because it might offend the sixteen West German students at the school.

One student, Tom Custer, seventeen, called a newspaper office, hoping the publicity would bring the school leaders to their senses.

Christine Kane, sixteen, complained to a *Philadelphia Inquirer* reporter, Suzanne Gordon: "They make us go to school, but then they say we have to learn this, but can't learn that."

The newly imposed dress code for juniors banned blue jeans, T-shirts, bare feet, and hats.

Petitions were started. Some football players shaved their heads in protest. The dress code was followed, but some, in protest, came very dressy or in outrageous outfits.

What do you think of this dress code?

Can you think of anything good about any dress code? What are some of the bad things?

Even without a dress code, are there pressures to look and dress like other people?

How about hairstyles? When is a hairstyle good, and when is it gross?

Is a hairstyle ever too gross? One year at Senn High School in Chicago, during annual funny hat day, one student wore a half dozen baby garter snakes in his makeshift hat. Live, they were all live! Is a class able.to study, if one student has live snakes in his or her hair or hat?

Should there be guidelines for—or a limit placed on—how everybody should look?

Well, the students at Swarthmore High got another surprise. The code and censorship were all a put-on, a way for the school leaders to show what it is like to live in a society of sudden and unfair rules. Classes in the school had been studying the censorship techniques of Nazi Germany, and the unfair labeling and rules of Senator Joseph McCarthy in the United States in the early 1950s. There was no code, after all, at Swarthmore!

But schools do have codes—for example, private schools or academies where students all wear the same style of clothing, usually of the same color. The advantages are that poor and rich kids "become" equal in appearance, and kids do not dress to vie with one another for attention. The disadvantage, of course, is that life is not very interesting when everyone looks alike.

But, dress code or no dress code, students look pretty much alike anyway. Says Dr. Tony Meade: "Kids wear T-shirts, with sports or rock slogans, jeans, tennis shoes—and they don't stray much from that."

For Rhonda Bastel, twelve, of Milburn Junior High in Overland Park, Kansas, it's a "regular" shirt or blouse, jeans or slacks, and Nike shoes or other tennis shoes. But one of her friends insists on coming to school in a dress, in a way breaking the popular, unwritten code. Is that weird? No, says Rhonda, "that person just likes wearing dresses, and that's nice. But I only wear them to a wedding or something, because weddings and stuff like that are nice, or maybe if we go out to eat, or Mother's Day or Christmas."

Thinking of fancy clothes lets us dream, and, in a way, to extend our personalities.

When you dream of new clothes, what do you dream? Kids at the Norristown (Pennsylvania) Eisenhower Middle School made lists of the kinds of clothes they would buy "if they had all the money in the world."

At their school, they have a dress code that bans gym or jogging suits, tube tops, shorts, and sweat jackets.

The Eisenhower students said they would like to buy towel shirts, designer jeans, leather sneakers, silk jackets, terry cloth shirts, preppy blouses, baggy pants, monogrammed sweaters, expensive tops, everything striped, satin jackets, Wrangler pants, pairs of Nikes or Pumas, some tuxes and a lot of suits, a sweet new jacket, some Sergios, Jordaches, Sassons.

Each of these tells us something about the person—that he or she is imaginative and wants to stand out and be different, for instance, or maybe that he or she doesn't.

One twelve-year-old boy at Eisenhower said that if he had all the money, he would only want to buy regular jeans and shirts, "nothing that fancy and expensive."

Dana Hull, twelve, of the Franklin Middle School, Reisterstown, Maryland, says: "Everyone worries about if what they wear is 'in.' I do, too. But you don't have to get everything that's the latest. Jeans are fine! Wear what you feel comfortable in."

Whether they dress simply or get a lot of attention by the way they dress, it is clear that kids want to be noticed by the way they dress and look. A big study of 10,000 students between fifth and ninth grade, and 15,000 parents, which is under way, shows, in the preliminary research, that young people are concerned about how they look to others. Larry Kalp, a member of the board that is conducting the "Study of Early Adolescents and Their Parents," funded by the Lilly Foundation, says the study so far is showing that "kids are evaluating their personal worth. They want to know 'How do I look?' It's a bigger thing than we thought. They are focusing on 'Who am I as a person?' "

Some try too hard to make an impression. A fashion notes article in the *Philadelphia Inquirer* (August 1, 1982) described the shopping habits of three women. The first went to different stores and bought a chic item at each store. Another decked herself out in one outfit of one designer. The boyfriends in each case did not seem unduly impressed. The first said, "It's hard to know who the real you is sometimes." The other said, "You always look nice. Is there something new?"

But the third woman only bought clothes that went with those she already owned. By putting various new and old pieces together, she created outfits that no one else would think of. One day, she put this year's jacket and shoes with last year's skirt and blouse, added her grandmother's art deco earrings and a new pair of lavender stockings. At her waist, she pinned a bunch of violets.

That night the person she cared about the most said: "You're amazing, you know. I never know what to expect, but you always look wonderful."

"The woman," according to designer Norma Kamali, "has to be the force that makes the outfit work."

Clothes are a kind of costuming, as for Halloween—you put on certain things to appear in a certain way or for effect, and sometimes, Halloween style, they do shock.

Although we might think that the clothing we wear depends on the weather, psychologist Robert Nicolay says: "Clothing really is a form of costuming. Clothes give impressions. See how I look? They may help us to slide into the background or be noticed. We costume ourselves to achieve an effect."

Sometimes we dress to annoy parents. Sometimes it is to impress our peer group.

You can walk into any high school and you'll see the "cool cats," "one of the guys," the "unique person," the "serious student," and so on.

The same with hair, says Dr. Nicolay. But hair is different. "You can't see how hair looks to others. People spend a lot of money on hair, for they don't know how it looks."

All that role-playing by looks is good, says Dr. Nicolay, but we need to change roles from time to time. He thinks that girls are better at that than boys, because they will change their hairdo, for instance. We all have to play a role, he says, but we don't want to spend too long on one role.

5

Too Mean to Laugh

What is a cult?

It is often a group that has split off from another group, and is usually tightly organized. A cult may also be run by a personality who exerts strong control over the members. In history, many a denomination or movement started as an offshoot group with a strong leader. In a sense, the Presbyterian, Methodist, Baptist, and other mainline churches started this way.

In some cases, cults are also very secretive, and this is true of many modern ones. They are often communal, that is, members share one another's goods. Some groups even rush pickup trucks to the home of a new member to claim all of the new member's belongings—bikes, records, stereo equipment, clothes. Eventually they even claim bank accounts.

In researching a book on cults—*The Far-Out Saints of the Jesus Communes*—this author concluded that there are good and bad cults. Some cults may become the denominations of the future. Most cults, however, are very fragile, depending on the personality of one demanding leader with an airtight lid on the minds of members. Except for noisy rituals, few cults have any sense of joy. And there are few questions—for they have all the answers.

How can you tell a good group from a bad group? It is wise to avoid any group that (1) has no sense of joy and (2) that has all the answers. Jesus himself said, "I have spoken thus to you, so that my joy may be in you, and your joy complete" (John 15:11), and he himself did not promise we would have all the answers: "But about that day and hour no one knows, not even the angels in heaven" (Matt. 24:36). And in his own moments of suffering, Jesus anguished on the cross, without an answer: "My God, my God, why hast thou forsaken me?" (Matt. 27:46).

Nevertheless, it is easy to be taken in by cult groups. Their members stand on school and university corners and promise peace of mind, love, and spiritual happiness versus unsatisfying worldly pursuits. Every young person should be cautious about bringers of new faiths who promise instant benefits.

In religious pursuit, as in shopping, it is best not to "buy" the first suit of new clothes dangled before you or the first pair of new shoes you see. Ask questions. Do some thinking. Check a few other "shops." Beware of the salesperson, whether he or she is selling insurance or religion, who wants you to buy sight unseen.

Delmar Wedel, director of international training for the YMCA of Greater New York, has a son who for six years has been inside one of the more lasting but controversial cults that began in Hollywood, California. Wedel sees his son on occasion, but wonders why he stays in the cult.

"He's not fulfilling his potential," Wedel says. "It's like a prison. The possibility of making judgments is difficult once you're in."

Then, the joyless, know-it-all attitude bothers Wedel. "The judgmental dimension is frightening. To them (the cult members), the righteous are a precious few. It must be kind of tiresome to feel the constant need to change other people. It must be exhausting."

How much should you let other people dominate your life? Should you take responsibility for changing the beliefs around you, and, if you feel it is important to do so (and the Scriptures do have this dimension), whom do you seek to change? People like yourself? People in a foreign land? People with beliefs really different from yours?

Over the years you will be asked to join different groups, clubs, and religious groups. What rules would you want to keep in mind as you make your decision in the face of bombardment and promotion by groups new to you?

Here is an outline for an imaginary novel on cults. It is modeled after real-life cults—the kind that might approach you someday. Some young people are fortunate to get out of heavy cults once they get in, some are not. See what happens to Mark:

LOVE'S SMILE

Chapter 1
Shelley and Mark are like two peas in a pod. She has short, red-auburn hair, blue eyes; he is tall, slim, with dark hair, and by nature is more quiet than she. Together they do a lot of funny things and have a great time. We see them going down the street, kidding each other, living it up. She is touched on the shoulder, but he jumps to the other side when she turns; she dances on the steps and lawn curbs; he imitates the school principal; they play with the animals; they buy identical funny T-shirts.

Chapter 2
The two kooky kids wander down the street hand in hand, meet and jest with friends, especially Shelley's close confidant, Jan, who is wowed by the T-shirts which have some crazy theme on them. They pass several unsmiling kids who have strange literature and are preaching their hearts out on some religious theme. It is clear later that these religious kids are way out in some far field. Nevertheless, Mark wants to listen. For a moment, there is even a hint that he is taking them seriously, which is a rare way for

Shelley or Mark to regard anything. Then, off go Shelley and Mark, skipping away in disco steps, waving at the humorless, now angry commune preachers.

Chapter 3
Shelley and her parents. Shelley has her hobbies, fun at home; she talks with Mark by phone. He's usually pretty smart without studying much, but he is concerned about a test. He sounds a little too serious and Shelley is not sure she likes that. She talks with Jan again and there is some rumor that Mark isn't going to make the team this year. Seems he and the coach don't get along. Shelley calls him back but he doesn't want to talk about it.

Chapter 4
Shelley and Jan and others at school. Activities. Lockers. "He's really acting weird." Jan: "He's always a little weird. . . . You too!" They laugh but they know something is happening to Mark. He's not his old fun self; he's distant.

Chapter 5
"He's gone. What do you mean? He can't leave just like that." Shelley meets with Mark's distraught parents; Mark, just recently turned eighteen and, legally accountable, has split; he took all his belongings, guitar, record collection, said he gave everything to the Forever House, which he has just joined. His note is an angry attack on his parents for living comfortable lives, a Scripture quote that says the chosen must forsake parents and all. Both families are in a panic over what to do. Attempts to get through to Mark in the Forever House are of no avail. Mark must be kept from the "world." Shelley is in tears. Her sorrow and Irish temper mix as she screams at her walls.

Chapter 6
Mark has dropped out of school. Shelley writes him letters, knows he's not receiving them. She walks by the communal house of the Forever movement. One day she encounters Mark, now thoroughly brainwashed, as he preaches on the street. He is cruel to her, glassy-eyed. He hurls Scriptures

at her: "Depart from me ye that work iniquity." She eventually screams at him and flees in tears.

Chapter 7
Shelley tries to forget Mark, meets some new friends, tries to be straight and simple one time and her old kooky self another; she does not fit in. She still loves Mark.

Chapter 8
The parents are not sitting idly by. They enlist a deprogrammer, who is about as mean as the cult members themselves, and they need Shelley and Jan and others to help.

Chapter 9
Shelley also visits with Ben Browne, a youth minister of a mainline denomination. He has his views on some of the new cults. He says something she doesn't forget: "Don't follow a group that has all the answers and that has no sense of joy, whose members do not know how to laugh." She liked that.

Chapter 10
The deprogramming effort is violent and negative. Mark is seized by a deprogramming task force, including his father and several football players, hustled off, sedated, and bombarded with words, just as he was when he was taken in by the Forever House. He appears to be coming out of it. Shelley screams at him along with the others.

Chapter 11
Mark at home. Thanksgiving Day. Mark is quiet, but he is not the former smiling Mark. He agrees with everybody, is closely eyed, as all seem to have a jovial familial time around him. Shelley mostly watches him. He talks a little, but after Thanksgiving dinner he disappears.

Chapter 12
Shelley seeks Mark out, gets his attention at the Forever House door. The leaders of the commune now make a point of indicating there is no problem (they know Mark is now well controlled). Shelley is mocked by Mark's attitude

and smirk, offended that his only interest is in converting her. She screams at him. They scream at each other. Farther than ever from him, she flees in defeat.

Chapter 13

Good friend Jan listens to Shelley, eventually picks up on the observation made by the youth minister earlier concerning the deficiencies of such groups. She wonders if a plan of attack could be made at these points. They meet with the youth minister; he likes the idea and the three of them develop a plan of action. If Mark doesn't have joy, let's bombard him somehow. Jan: "Shelley, you do that," and Jan has some ideas. The youth minister is going to challenge Mark at every turn with Scripture, in order to confront the authoritarian stance of Mark's group. They enlist teachers and friends to send birthday and other thoughtful cards. Is all of this too mawkish, too impractical? Jan: "You got to do something."

Chapter 14

So they do their thing. The attempt to undermine the authority of the group by the youth minister fails as Mark asserts his own Scripture. Mark ends up angry, refusing to talk or argue. The thoughtful cards are ignored, regarded as patronizing and phony, from people who never sent cards before.

Shelley walks back and forth by the commune every day. Mark doesn't want to see her. She keeps it up. She always makes a point of doing funny things, including her funny dances, her funny facial imitations, anything she can think of that is funny. She has a feeling she is on a stage by herself in a very lonely world. One day, when the sun is bright, and the winter air brisk, she is outside the commune again. She dances up and down the sidewalk. She thinks she catches a glimpse of Mark in the window. The tempo of her dancing steps up; she uses all her funny steps. Suddenly, she slips on a sliver of ice, turns head over heels. She gets up. She's OK, shrugs her shoulders, laughs and continues her dancing. Worn out, she slows a little. She hears the door open, glances back slightly, and catches a glimpse of Mark putting on a jacket. She keeps up her little dances, until she feels a couple of gentle hands cover her eyes and hears "Guess who?" "I don't know," she says coyly, continuing to move slowly. At the corner, her lips and Mark's touch, there is a forever embrace, and they walk away, each one very much part of the other, as hostile shouts of "Brother Mark! Brother Mark!" fade behind them.

DEATH

6

"Some Other Dawn"

"The Associated Press reports carrying the news of Mary White's death declared that it came as the result of a fall from a horse. How she would have hooted at that! She never fell from a horse in her life. Horses have fallen on her and with her—'I'm always trying to hold 'em in my lap,' she used to say. . . . Her death resulted not from a fall but from a blow on the head which fractured her skull, and the blow came from the limb of an overhanging tree. . . ."

So begins one of the most famous editorials in an American newspaper. It was May 1921, and noted editor William Allen White, of Emporia, Kansas, was writing in his newspaper, the *Gazette,* about the accidental death of his sixteen-year-old daughter, Mary White.

Do you feel you know Mary, as you read on in his editorial?

"The last hour of her life was typical of its happiness. She came home from a day's work at school, topped off by a hard grind with the copy on the High School Annual, and felt that a ride would refresh her. She climbed into her khakis . . . and hurried to get her horse and be out on the dirt roads for the country air and the radiant green fields of the spring. As she rode through the town on an easy gallop, she kept waving at passers-by. She knew everyone in town. For a decade the little figure in the long pigtail and the red hair ribbon has been familiar on the streets of Emporia. . . .

"She never had a 'date,' nor went to a dance, except once with her brother Bill. . . . But young people—great spring-breaking, varnish-cracking, fender-bending, door-sagging carloads of 'kids'—gave her great pleasure. Her zests were keen. . . . She joined the church. . . . She felt the church was an agency for helping people to more of life's abundance, and she wanted to help. She never wanted help for herself. . . . She was a Peter Pan who refused to grow up.

"Her funeral yesterday at the Congregational Church was as she would have wished it; no singing, no flowers except the big bunch of red roses from her brother Bill's Harvard classmen—heavens, how proud that would have made her! And the red roses from the *Gazette* forces, in vases, at her head and feet. . . .

"It would have made her smile to know that her friend, Charley O'Brien, the traffic cop, had been transferred from Sixth and Commercial to the corner near the church to direct her friends who came to bid her good-by.

"A rift in the clouds in a gray day threw a shaft of sunlight upon her coffin as her nervous, energetic little body sank to its last sleep. But the soul of her, the glowing, gorgeous, fervent soul of her, surely was flaming in eager joy upon some other dawn." (Emporia [Kansas] *Gazette*, May 17, 1921)

What do you know about Mary, her parents, her friends?
If it's true that you learn from life, is it also true that you learn from death, from the death of an acquaintance or a loved one?
What might you remember about a person when he or she dies?
How should you feel when someone dies? How should you act? Should you cry? How much?
Why do people feel guilty when someone dies?

You may not think about death much, but it is there. Some 160,000 persons die every day in this country.

Chances are you have had some experience with death—of a grandparent, a friend, a neighbor. When you add up the experiences of death by all those around you, death certainly seems more of a reality.

Here are some experiences with death reported by kids from Carol Quackenbush's Blue Springs (Missouri) Junior High School eighth-grade class:

—"I did lose my best friend when I was almost fourteen and soon after we started in eighth grade. My friend came to school for three days and at the beginning of September to mid-October my friend lay in a hospital, looking better, so they thought. I was going to see my friend one October night, but I was told during my lunch hour period that she died early that morning. I was told that she literally looked like skin and bones. I told them I could handle it. I was so upset, but I believe that God didn't want me to see her while she was alive. My friend died of diabetes and C.F. (cystic fibrosis). I didn't even cry at her funeral. I just held it all in, because I was so upset. I still and probably never will understand everything that happened. One thing that still upsets me is nobody will believe that she was my best friend."—Girl, 14.

—"When my grandmother died I thought the world was coming to an end. I was only seven years old at her time of death. I had been so close to her. Why did she have to go? I really never knew my grandma real well. Only the super times we shared. I loved her very much. Now she's gone. Life goes on always. Seven years later, I have one grandpa, and one grandma left. I remember so little about her. I want to remember her just the way she was. I love her very much."—Boy, 14.

—"About a year ago my grandfather died. I remember just sort of having the feeling he was going to when he was sick. I wasn't real close to him, but he was my grandpa. I never saw him very often either. I was sad he died and all, but I never really cried. I felt bad that I couldn't cry. It made me feel guilty that I just couldn't. I miss him, but it's like I expect him to walk in the room when I'm at my grandmother's. I kind of feel like all the violence and death on television makes you immune to the violence and death in real life."—Boy, 14.

—"Just recently my great-uncle died and my grandma has been lost without him. Since I knew him for such a short time, I really didn't know what to feel like when he died. All through the visitation and funeral my grandmother cried. Somehow I don't think she's going to make it by herself. Nobody knows what to do or say to make her feel better. People sure mean a lot."—Boy, 13.

—"I don't remember very much. I was six. I woke up on Sunday morning, and was getting ready for church. When Dad came in and said Grandpa died, my only response was 'Which one?' After, I finally grasped what happened. I bawled all day."—Girl, 14.

—"Before my grandma died, that was a year ago, she lived in a nursing home. She had cancer in her lungs and she wasn't very healthy. Her legs were all swollen up and she had to keep this oxygen thing over her mouth for air. One night my other grandma and aunt were in her room and before she died she told them she loved them. She died peacefully, but it was a sad time for everybody, even me, because she could make everybody love her."—Girl, 14.

—"This girl in my P.E. class had a cousin whom she liked a lot and who would do anything for her. (He was about nineteen.) He had a broken hand and was cleaning his gun. He dropped it and it shot him in the head. His last words to his mom were, 'Say good-by to _____ (the girl) for me.' The girl was sad but I never saw her cry. She didn't miss any school and the whole time she seemed almost happy."—Girl, 14.

—"My aunt lost my cousin, her son, and he was only

sixteen but he died in a motorcycle wreck in Dallas, Texas. The weird thing is that my grandma had a dream the night before the accident that Steve was going to have a wreck and get killed. And the next day that's what happened."— Boy, 14.

—"My aunt was real close to me. She had cancer. They said she might die about five years ago. She lived about three more years. Then she went into the hospital. The cancer was spreading and she had a lot of pain. I didn't want her to die, but I didn't want her to go through any more pain. She died though, and she was glad that she did."—Boy, 14.

—"My grandma died two years ago and my mom was crying all the time, but I hardly ever cried. I just knew she went to heaven with my mom's dad and her mom and dad."—Boy, 14.

—"One day I woke up and my mom told me that someone found my aunt on the bottom step dead. She had been feeding her cat when she just died. She was still sitting up leaning against a railing when she died. I'm kinda glad she died early in the morning cause she didn't suffer at all. At least she didn't suffer. I wish she was here today, though."—Girl, 13.

In a way, it's helpful to know that we are not alone in a time of death. Everyone else has similar experiences.

"Life is a cycle," says a worker with handicapped children, Dr. Doris E. Hadary of American University, Washington, D.C. "Life never ends." And death is a part of that cycle. Some believe, as Christians, that the cycle goes into eternity. Some believe the cycle brings a person's love and will on to others.

"Death is almost final, but not quite," says Dr. James Cone, a theologian at Union Theological Seminary, New York. "I believe in the resurrection. Death is the only way one can be resurrected."

It's not necessary really to understand death, any more than it is necessary to understand everything in the universe.

"What is your understanding of death?" asks Buff Bradley in his book *Endings: A Book About Death* (Addison-Wesley, 1979). "Maybe you don't have a single, clear attitude toward death; maybe what you have is a whole goulash of feelings and ideas. Maybe one week you think one way about death, and the next week you think another, and the week after that you don't know what to think at all. It takes much living and thinking and feeling to come to some kind of big understanding about death. You'll probably experience a lot of confusion, and fear, before you develop an understanding that seems right and real to you. You'll learn from other people and perhaps make some of their ideas your own. But when it comes right down to it, your understanding of death is completely personal, all your own. Even if you accept somebody else's understanding, you're the one who decides, all alone, in the privacy of your mind."

Even though we cannot expect to understand fully death (or life), there are some things that help us face the death of loved ones.

Kids in Audrey Brainard's sixth-grade class at Cedar Drive School, Colts Neck, New Jersey, have also experienced the death of a grandparent, aunt, or other family member.

They offer these ways to deal with sadness in time of death:

1. Comfort others involved.
2. Keep your mind off the subject.
3. Do something the person who died would like.
4. Say to yourself it happened and there's nothing you can do about it.
5. Cry your head off in your room.

6. Do something that is fun.
7. Read a book.
8. Get a pet.
9. Spend some time praying.
10. Rest and relax.

New York psychologist Dr. Salvatore Didato suggests: Try writing your feelings out, if it is too painful to express them in spoken words. Then ask your mother or father to discuss them with you.

In his book *Psychotechniques: How to Help Yourself or Someone You Love* (Methuen, 1980), Dr. Didato also suggests:

1. "Don't isolate yourself. Even though you may not feel like it, keep up your contacts with people. Socialize with others, and stay close to family members. Allow yourself to be consoled. Let emotion out, don't hold back, and don't reject offers from someone you like who wants to help distract you from your sadness. Permit yourself to lean on them a bit more at this time.

2. "Fatigue and poor physical health will definitely deepen your melancholy. So avoid exhaustion, loss of sleep, and overwork. This is a time when you must conserve your energy and keep as healthy as possible. Many people find it helpful to take hot baths, long walks, massages, and do gentle exercises. Try to eat nourishing meals and get plenty of rest and relaxation.

3. "Stay away from morbid situations. Don't go in for 'heavy' movies or TV shows, or lectures or sullen topics. This rule applies socially as well. Avoid people who have a pessimistic nature and are themselves morose or angry. Rather, associate with those you know who, in the past, have given you a 'lift,' those who are optimistic and have a cheerful disposition."

Dr. Didato also points out that most people who have lost a loved one have a sense of guilt—about something they did wrong or didn't appreciate before the person died. This is normal. "Decide that there is only one reality about the past—that *nothing can be done to change it*," says Dr. Didato. A person, however, can "atone," or make up for mistakes, by doing something that would please the deceased. "A teenager who lost his sister in a car accident took an oath never to speed again. And a young woman whose little brother drowned vowed to give time each summer to teach children to swim."

EMBARRASSMENT

7

It's Not So Funny!

The teen stood in front of a big group in the basement of the North Shore Baptist Church in Chicago. The audience included church leaders who were quite prominent in the community, among them James L. Kraft, the founder of the Kraft Foods Company.

The occasion was an oratorical contest for teens sponsored by the church. First prize was an all-expense-paid trip to a beautiful camp at Green Lake, Wisconsin. The second prize was a free week at camp, but with no transportation allowance.

Henry probably should not have been in the contest. He was shy, spoke haltingly. But he was game and really prepared. His speech was a "one, two, three" type, and he had all the points memorized. Only, when Henry got to the third point, he forgot it. He kept holding up three fingers for the third point, but it was only after terrible agonizing that he got the third point out. Of course, he was embarrassed.

But some good came out of it: Henry did win second place, a week at the camp in Wisconsin. (He rode his bicycle two hundred miles to get there.) And James L. Kraft, a kindly aging man, became his friend. Henry could be seen, on occasion, in a chauffeur-driven limousine with the old man as they went to dinner in an expensive restaurant. And Henry could walk past all the corporation executives, past the secretaries, past the life-size portrait of Kraft, into his office. Later, while a college student, Henry kept house at the magnificent Kraft mansion in Wilmette, Illinois.

The same Henry, now a writer and editor, remembers another embarrassing experience while a freshman at William Jewell College in Liberty, Missouri.

A waiter, Henry became pretty good at balancing trays of food in the college dining hall. Only this time, Henry, in white waiter coat, was carrying four big bowls of juicy beets on his tray. Henry slipped. You guessed it. Henry landed in the middle of the dining hall floor with bowls of dark beet juice dripping all over him. There was a thunderous roar of laughter. Can you think of a more embarrassing moment?

What was your most embarrassing moment?
It probably wasn't funny to you then. As you look back now, was it funny?
When is an embarrassment funny, and when isn't it?
Is it possible to do embarrassing things, and not be embarrassed?
Is it good to be embarrassed? What about a person who never gets embarrassed? Would you like him or her?
How many ways of being embarrassed can you think of?

Students in Alice Cortner's ninth- and tenth-grade classes at the Clarksville (Tennessee) Academy, a private school, were asked about their most embarrassing moments.

Which of these stories do you think are the funniest? Why? Which are not so funny?

What do you think a person should do in each of these cases?

—"When I was in the seventh grade I was a cheerleader. Once, at a game, all the other cheerleaders went out on the floor to do a cheer and left me up in the stands. All the others were out there except me. You could tell I was missing, because there was an empty space in the line-up."—Girl, 15.

—"One day in the cheerleading practice we were learning a new routine. I was having trouble learning all of the motions, and none of the other cheerleaders would help me. I understand that I don't catch on as quickly as some of the others, but what I can't understand is why they wouldn't help me. Halfway through practice these guys, football players to be exact, came in to watch. All the other cheerleaders wanted to show them the routines. I didn't, because one of the football players and I had been out on a date. Well, the cheerleaders started to do the routine and sure enough I messed up. That was embarrassing in itself. But what added to it more was that the other cheerleaders screamed and really got mad at me for messing up. They even screamed at me in front of the guy I had been dating. I was really embarrassed."—Girl, 15.

—"On a rainy day, I was running into the cafeteria, because I didn't want to get wet. My shoes were wet, which made the bottom slick. As I ran through the door, I slid across the room and fell down right in front of the teachers."—Girl, 14.

—"On the bus riding home one time my hair got really filled with static electricity and stood out in every direction and everyone was laughing at me. I put on my head a wool cap and someone pulled it off and it just got worse."—Boy, 14.

—"I was in the school chorus and we were preparing to put on a show at the athletic awards banquet. I was one of the five main dancers. Thinking that this would be fine, I practiced with the chorus. I am not a bad singer. We began to put dance to the music and we practiced every day. I skipped several of the practice sessions and with one week before the performance I was still stumbling and people began to laugh. My peers were good from practice and I was lousy and I was embarrassed."—Boy, 15.

—"One time when I was in first grade I went over to a friend's house. We were playing outside in the mud and got our clothes dirty. My friend's older sister gave us the idea of taking our clothes off. When we did we wrapped towels around us. Her sister then dared us to go streaking around the house. We did. There was a boy across the street that I didn't know. He saw us but didn't know who I was. Later on he started to go to our school and he always remembered me because of the streaking."—Girl, 15.

—"It was my first year of middle school basketball. I didn't get to play much. We had a second string game toward the end of the year. Unluckily I was third string. Finally I got to go into the game. Now picture this. Our bench was on a stage about a foot high. I tripped and over the side I went. Onto the gym floor I lay."—Boy, 15.

—"When I did terrible on a math test, the test was to see who got to go to the math contest and everybody did OK on it except me. I did terrible."—Boy, 14.

—"I had to read something in front of the school, and when I was doing it I kept on messing up on this one word. I felt like I was as dumb as a second-grader. The people smiled and laughed at me. And when I went over and sat down I just smiled."—Boy, 15.

—"I was spending the night with a friend and it was getting late. We went to bed and you see I'm allergic to certain types of beds. I lay down and I began to feel it coming on. My reaction to this is I actually have an accident in the bed. So I tried my best to stay awake but I failed. And sometime during the night it happened. And the next morning I woke up wet. The bed was wet and so was I. I got up and got dressed quickly, trying to act like nothing happened. But it didn't work. A thirteen-year-old wetting the bed. Only babies do that."—Boy, 14.

—"When I was small, I don't remember how old I was, but we went to the Smoky Mountains on vacation and went to Cherokee Village. My family and I were watching an

Indian dance and the Chief said, ' Come, Little Brave, and dance with us.' I thought he said little boy, but he was really talking to another Indian there. Anyway, I went running to the car and hid in the back seat. When my dad came and asked me what was wrong, I told him, and he explained what happened."—Boy, 14.

—"When I was in the seventh grade, I was in a play called *Monster Madness.* I played a lead role as 'tombstone,' At the start of the play all the lights were turned off, so I could not find my way to the tombstone. When the lights finally came on, I found myself standing in the middle of the floor like a total jerk. I slowly made my way to the tombstone and the play went on fine. The thing about it was that very few people in the crowd knew that I was supposed to be at the tombstone. Most of the people figured that it was just part of the show, but I still felt it inside, and still do today."—Boy, 16.

—"I was out in the yard. Dad was seeding the yard. He asked me to bring my tractor to pack down the seed (drive over it). The tractor wasn't in the best shape, and it wouldn't go in the yard without spinning a wheel. Dad didn't like this a bit, and he yelled and yelled and griped at me. Of course, there was nothing I could do to prevent the spinning. There were neighbors out in the yards everywhere that day, so I was embarrassed. I felt the neighbors thought of me as a fool, when I was not! All of them heard him, and some of the words weren't clean! I was ashamed to walk down the street. Some might say, 'There comes that boy from the yard across the street!' "—Boy, 15.

This last boy says he fights embarrassment by "trying to pretend that I am not embarrassed."

Some of the others agree and add, "Just try to laugh it off along with everyone else." Others in the same group say:

—"When I am embarrassed I just am quiet, because I don't want to make my embarrassment worse."

—"It doesn't matter what other people think. They look just as stupid other times, too."

—"I leave the room (not in anger)."

—"If embarrassed by one's sister or parent, avoid being with them in public. In short, avoid the situation."

—"Usually I try to make a snappy comeback or just play along with the situation. It is good to accept it and make a joke out of it."

Five face-saving tips are suggested by Dr. Julius Segal and Zelda Segal in *Seventeen* magazine (April 1980) in an article on "How to Handle Embarrassment":

1. *Acknowledge your slipup.* It doesn't help to try to cover up in an embarrassing situation. If, for example, you can't remember an acquaintance's name, it's better to admit that you've forgotten than to try bluffing your way through an awkward exchange.

2. *Don't focus on the symptoms.* The more you struggle to mask your blushing, perspiring, or heart palpitations, the more troublesome they are likely to become. Instead, try taking a few deep breaths and dealing with the *situation* that caused your discomfort rather than the *symptoms* accompanying it.

3. *Try to see the humor.* Nobody likes to take a pratfall in a crowd, but such situations are funny. It helps to acknowledge the humor in an embarrassing situation—even to join in the laughter.

4. *Go on with your day.* Don't allow an embarrassing incident to ruin your plans for a scheduled event—be it a dinner party, a date, or a classroom presentation. Fleeing the scene will only increase your discomfort. Stick with your plans and accept the episode as just one minor blip on an otherwise bright screen.

5. *Don't brood about the episode.* Often, we give an embarrassing incident far greater weight than it warrants. It doesn't help to dwell on an episode everyone else has forgotten.

Some people like to embarrass other people. "I see a lot of this," says Tony Meade of the Institute for Juvenile Research in Chicago. "Some people like to make people feel bad. They see putting people down has an impact, like fighting. It makes one's own self look good and gives a sense of power. The powerful person is one who can put another down."

Teasing is a part of this technique of putting a person down. If you can't think of an answer to someone who is teasing you, you may feel put out. There is more than one appropriate response: you may want to ignore it; or you may want to laugh with the person; or you may realize it won't hurt you to be put down and humbled a little once in a while. When you feel embarrassed, think about it.

8

More than a Dog

Complete this quiz:

1. A friend is somebody who will always tell you something nice. True or False.
2. A friend is somebody you can have all to yourself, and you don't have to share. True or False.
3. A friend is always cheery around you. True or False.
4. A friend will never get you into trouble. True or False.
5. A friend will wait for you, even hours, if you are shopping or at a movie. True or False.

If you're talking about human friends, then probably all these should be false.

In the first case, your friend who would always say nice things would be a tape recorder, repeating your own voice.

In the second case, a friend you don't have to share could be a stuffed toy.

In the third case, a friend that is always cheery around you is a doll that speaks when you pull the cord.

In the fourth case, a friend that will never get you into trouble might be a robot.

In the fifth case, a friend that will wait long hours for you is probably a dog, "man's best friend," tied to the door.

Your friends who are people will never be perfect. To enjoy friends, you have to listen to some good advice from them once in a while, share them with others, help them when they are unhappy, maybe even get in trouble helping or standing up for them, and not expect too much from them, such as waiting around a long time for you.

A friend is somebody you like—and trust. If you like the friend, you will do things for that person and share with him or her. If you trust a friend, you may get suggestions and ideas worth listening to that others might not tell you.

How do you define a friend?

"A friend is one who dislikes the same people that you dislike," says one unknown ancient writer.

Aristotle, the Greek philosopher, said, "A true friend is one soul in two bodies."

Ralph Waldo Emerson, nineteenth-century writer and philosopher, told us, "A friend may well be reckoned the masterpiece of nature."

Claude Mermet said: "Friends are like melons. Shall I tell you why? To find one good, you must a hundred try."

George Eliot, in *The Spanish Gypsy*, talked of a "friend more divine than all divinities."

Michael Vitkovics, in *Love and Friendship*, wrote: "Friendship is the holiest of gifts; God can bestow nothing more sacred upon us."

How is your definition of a friend different from these? Would you add anything?

Can you think of a book about friends you have read? How were the two friends alike or different? Why were they friends?

In the Bible there is the famous story of the friendship of David and Jonathan (I Sam. 18). Jonathan was the quiet son of a king, Saul; David was the sling-wielding slayer of giants and a boy who was well on his way to becoming a king himself. How could the two young men be friends? Why?

Can you think of a better definition of friendship than the one Jesus gave: "There is no greater love than this, that a man should lay down his life for his friends." (John 15:13)

When the big 737 jetliner bound for Florida crashed into a crowded bridge that linked Washington, D.C., and Virginia, in 1982, and settled into the icy depths of the Potomac, one man pulled several people to the safety ropes of a helicopter, then sank into the water himself, giving his life for them. In the summer of 1982, a Willow Grove, Pennsylvania, man died trying to save an eleven-year-old boy felled by a high voltage wire grounded in a violent storm. Were the people these two died for their friends?

In some ways, all people are your friends. A young man who dies for his country is saying that the people of his land are his friends. There are also stories of people dying to save their enemies. In the movie *Blade Runner,* Harrison Ford (who also played in *Star Wars* and *Raiders of the Lost Ark*) is hunting androids to kill, but in the end an android, who is dying, spares Ford's life. The idea of peace in the world is based on the idea that all men are brothers or friends.

Friends do not come easy. Certainly with people still killing one another in war and crime, the ideal of friendship of all is far away, if not impossible.

So, we have friends one by one. They are the individuals we can share with and do things with and get along with. Even so, we have to work at it.

Here is how psychologists and educators tell us we can work at having friends:

1. Be a good listener. Don't interrupt others.
2. Don't talk too much about yourself. Don't brag.
3. Don't believe all you hear about another. Find out yourself what a person is like.
4. Enjoy another's success. Don't be jealous.
5. Go where people are—ball games, club groups, meetings.
6. Be honest. Don't be nice just to make people like you.

7. Give and take. Be willing to take your share of criticism.

8. Share—that includes things such as cookies and popcorn, and also your ideas.

9. Keep your promises, and the secrets entrusted to you.

10. Talk with others about what you have in common.

11. Don't judge people by the way they look, how much money they have, or how popular they are.

12. Avoid getting angry. Apologize when you are wrong.

Dr. Joseph R. Novello, who conducts a talk show on problems of youngsters on radio in Washington, D.C., says, if you don't have friends, sit back and ask why. If other kids don't like you or if they call you names, figure out why. Are you more anxious to get than to give? Is there something you do to turn off other people? Work on correcting that trait and being likable. Then, secondly, he says, "go on a friend hunt. Pick out a person you would like to be with and look for things you both like. And, one friend leads to another."

Kids in Suzan Young Bramley's fifth-grade class at the Buckingham (Pennsylvania) Elementary School were asked to "think of somebody who doesn't have a friend or many friends. Why don't they have friends?"

The kids said that the people they knew who had no friends were: "Mean, big, dumb, knows everything, thinks everybody likes her (or him), talks about others, isn't true to others, looks ugly and gets into fights, teases other people, steals, is very tough, doesn't try to make new friends, is a bad sport, bothers people, makes stupid jokes, brags, isn't adjustable, is not very nice to some people, calls people names, cries easily, is a smart mouth, bully, big shot, weird, cheats, bosses others, acts like a baby, is unfair, smells, is very grumpy, likes to push people around." So who want to be friends with them?

Some kids like to have "best" friends, some don't. Says an eleven-year-old girl in the sixth grade at the Westtown Friends School, Westtown, Pennsylvania: "I think that I need some breathing space. I don't want a very thick friend. Someone I tell *everything* to would be a best friend, and I don't want a best friend, just a lot of very good ones."

Said a twelve-year-old at the same school: "Friends aren't always good for you, because sometimes they get you into trouble for something you didn't do."

How do you tell a good friend from a bad friend? The Buckingham kids said:

1. A good friend doesn't make fun of you.
2. A good friend doesn't hurt you.
3. A good friend keeps secrets and shares secrets with you.
4. A good friend shares.
5. A good friend understands you.
6. A good friend sticks up for you.
7. A good friend doesn't want money or gifts.
8. A good friend stays your friend even though you have other friends.
9. A good friend has a hobby or interest like yours.
10. A good friend is one you can talk to outright without being scared he'll get mad.
11. A good friend is cheerful—not the whining type.
12. A good friend listens to you.

Said one of the Buckingham students, a girl, ten: "If that friend is real friendly, then *that* is a good friend!"

HEALTH: BODY AND MIND

9

A Ten-Day Test

It was 607 B.C. and the city of Jerusalem surrendered. The proud conqueror, Nebuchadnezzar, of Babylon, a great city in what is Iraq today, sent his troops in, took away the riches of the Temple and the city, and proceeded to build himself a great palace.

Among the prisoners taken back to Babylon were the young Daniel and other princes of Judah. They were in such splendid physical shape that Nebuchadnezzar wanted to reeducate them to be useful to him. They were "young men of good looks and bodily without fault, at home in all branches of knowledge, well informed, intelligent, and fit for service in the royal court" (Dan. 1:4). They were to learn the Chaldean language of their captors and eat "a daily allowance of food and wine from the royal table" (Dan. 1:4–5).

That was the problem. Daniel and his friends were always careful about what they ate. They drew their strength from carefully selected vegetables.

Daniel was determined not to contaminate himself by touching the food and wine assigned to him by the king. He said to the guard in charge of Hananiah, Mishael, Azariah, and himself, " 'Submit us to this test for ten days. Give us only vegetables to eat and water to drink; then compare our looks with those of the young men who have lived on the food assigned by the king, and be guided in

your treatment of us by what you see.' The guard listened
to what they said and tested them for ten days. At the end
of ten days they looked healthier and were better nour-
ished than all the young men who had lived on the food
assigned them by the king. So the guard took away the
assignment of food and the wine they were to drink, and
gave them only the vegetables." (Dan. 1:8–16)

Then there is this story about a popular comedy star,
John Belushi, a very funny man in movies such as *Animal
House, The Blues Brothers,* and *Neighbors:*

> LOS ANGELES, March 10 (UPI)—John Belushi died of
> an overdose of heroin and cocaine, Dr. Thomas T.
> Noguchi, the Los Angeles County Coroner, said today.
>
> "The medical investigation into the death of John
> Belushi has been completed," Dr. Noguchi said in a brief
> statement. "The deceased died of an overdose of heroin
> and cocaine.
>
> "Both cocaine and heroin were found on the premis-
> es," Dr. Noguchi said.
>
> There have been numerous reports that the thirty-
> three-year-old Mr. Belushi had died of an overdose of
> cocaine, but the coroner's statement was the first men-
> tion of heroin.
>
> Mr. Belushi, the manic, irreverent comedian who rose
> to fame on the *Saturday Night Live* television series, was
> found dead in bed in his bungalow at the Chateau
> Marmont Hotel last Friday. (*New York Times,* March 11,
> 1982)

What do these two stories have in common?
*What kind of stuff do you put into your body? Anything that
might not be good for it?*
*Which is more important to take care of? Your body or your
mind?*
"You pay for everything in life. Either now or later." This

view from a famous minister, Harry Emerson Fosdick, could mean that early education and training helps to get the better jobs in later life. What else can it mean?

What is meant by the slogan, "You are what you eat"?

Most people want to feel good, look good, and be appealing to other people. Good health, of course, is one way of achieving those goals. What are some of the things you can do to keep your health in tiptop shape?

If you're going to be "healthy, wealthy, and wise," look at people who are. Look at people who are smart and see how they got that way. Look at people who are rich. What steps did they take in life? Look at the healthy, the athletic, the guy or girl with strength and sparkling eyes.

Young people in schools in Minnesota and New York State were asked: "Tell about the healthiest person you know—how did he or she get that way?"

"The healthiest person I know," says one girl in the seventh grade at Hosterman Junior High School, New Hope, Minnesota, "eats well, jogs, and stays fit. He doesn't eat stuff that has a lot of cholesterol or sugar." This girl says she roller-skates, swims, jogs, plays tennis, bikes, and hikes.

Said a boy, thirteen, another Hosterman student: "The healthiest person I know gets that way because he or she gets a lot of exercise, eats right, gets enough sleep, doesn't smoke, drink, or take drugs, and gets along with others."

At the John T. Roberts Elementary School in Syracuse, New York, a girl, eleven, said: "The healthiest person I know is well built, young, beautiful, nice, and they got that way by eating good foods and drinking good liquids." Another eleven-year-old at the same school: "I know a person that is healthy and he jogs every morning and he's a gym teacher. He does sit-ups every morning. He's really in shape."

Dr. Charles L. Bassman, a young clinical psychologist

who deals with kids in Marlton, New Jersey, reports that a lot of kids are into helping their own bodies. They say to him: "I'm not going to let that happen to my body." They see drugs appearing to work for some older kids, and they can't be scared from drugs. But when it comes down to taking care of their bodies, they can see the realities of drugs, alcohol, smoking, junk food and other things abusing the body."

As to smoking, Tony Meade at the Institute for Juvenile Research in Chicago says that kids have clearly got the message on smoking and its effects, partly from the anti-smoking ads on television. "What can be pointed out is that pot (marijuana) smoking has the same effects on lungs as nicotine."

A doctor, Donald P. Tashkin, of the UCLA School of Medicine in Los Angeles puts it this way:

"The habitual deep inhalation of marijuana into the lungs has the potential for injuring the respiratory tract and inducing lung cancer, as suggested by the following evidence. The principle active ingredient in marijuana, 9-tetra-hydrocannabinol (THC), is itself irritating to the respiratory tract. In addition to THC, marijuana contains essentially the same respiratory irritants that are found in tobacco, as well as 50 percent more carcinogenic hydrocarbons. A few laboratory studies have actually demonstrated respiratory tract injury in experimental animals and malignant transformation in cultured lung cells following chronic exposure to marijuana smoke." (In Leonard Gross's *The Parents' Guide to Teenagers*)

As to cigarette smoking, a study in 1964 by the U.S. Surgeon General's Advisory Committee on Smoking and Health surprised the country with its scientific findings that smoking is related to lung cancer and that cigarette smoking is "the most important of the causes of chronic bronchitis in the United States . . . (and) increases the risk of dying from chronic bronchitis and emphysema."

Congress proceeded to order each cigarette package and each printed advertisement to carry this warning. "The Surgeon General Has Determined That Cigarette Smoking Is Dangerous to Your Health." Cigarette advertising is banned on radio and television.

Other studies show that cigarette smoking increases the pressure of blood in the arteries and makes the heart work harder, endangering people with high blood pressure or weak hearts. And, warns Arnold Madison in *Smoking and You* (Messner, 1975), "if the arteries are already contracted by nicotine, they may close off completely. Clogged arteries can affect your brain, your hearing and your vision."

Researchers in 1982 began to suggest a link between smoking and cancers other than lung cancer. In a letter to the *New England Journal of Medicine,* Dr. R. T. Ravenholt, director of world health surveys for the Center for Disease Control, said small radioactive particles in cigarette smoke—already linked to lung cancer—may also be the source of malignant tumors elsewhere in the bodies of heavy smokers. Ravenholt said in an Associated Press interview that "the American public is exposed to far more radiation from the smoking of tobacco than they are from any other source or indeed from any other sources combined." Ravenholt and other researchers point out that a person who smokes a pack and a half a day takes in a yearly dose of alpha radiation equal to three hundred chest X-rays (*Philadelphia Inquirer,* July 29, 1982).

Asked what advice they would give other kids, students in Margrette Davis' sixth-grade class at the Florida A & M University High School (FAMU), Tallahassee, Florida, said drugs "are dangerous; they could kill you; you won't be normal; they could make you kill yourself; they'll get you in trouble." Said one boy, eleven: "I would remind kids how effective it (use of drugs) is. How it can harm the body. Ask what purpose it serves. Tell them to watch out for pushers. And say no to anyone who offers drugs." And there's good reason for such advice.

Among the drugs that can mess up your body easily is LSD, which is produced from ergot, a fungus that grows on rye and other grains. The name comes from the chemical term lysergic acid diethylamide. LSD mixes up the senses. A blinking of lights might come through as sound, such as bells; a pinprick as an explosion of lights, or music as color, says Margaret Hyde in *Mind Drugs* (McGraw-Hill, 1981). Paranoia—excessive, unreal fears— may develop and cause panic.

Amphetamines (pep pills) are chemical stimulants and include a host of drugs, including Methedrine, or "speed." They bring on hallucinations or wild visions. The user may not sleep for several days and seldom eats. Acute mental problems may result.

Cocaine ("coke") comes from leaves of a South American shrub, *Erythroxylon coca*, and, like amphetamines, affects the central nervous system. Cocaine can cause extreme anxiety, convulsions, and psychosis.

Barbiturates ("goofballs") depress the general nervous system and are used by doctors to help people sleep. The effects of these sedatives are much like alcohol—slurred speech, slowed thinking and response, exaggeration in some actions.

Heroin ("smack"), from poppies, is a "suicidal" kind of drug. It demands dependence that destroys a person's life as one steals and commits other crimes to acquire more.

Phencyclidine (PCP), "angel dust," a newer drug, is an anesthetic. It has a mellowing, "spaced out" effect. Users may have to hold on to buildings as they walk down a narrow street. They usually cannot do schoolwork or other activities.

And, of course, alcohol, an anesthetic, is the most prominently used drug. Some 95 million persons in the

United States are users, 9 million of them alcoholics—one out of ten.

Twenty-four percent of the American people polled by Gallup in 1978 said that alcohol had caused a bad effect in some way on their lives. Of the adult population, 71 percent drink and 47 percent had no guidelines or rules for drinking. Why one becomes an alcoholic is not fully understood. Certainly if one is to drink, he or she will need to impose limits and look for danger signs of dependence.

Hyde suggests that one way to avoid drugs is to seek better alternatives. Think about the kind of drug that is being used around you. What does it promise? If it promises quietness or mystical experience, meditation groups and Eastern religious disciplines can achieve these more safely.

If you want acceptance by a group, then seek out other groups or people who are not drug users, such as in churches and social centers. If it is intellectual stimulus you want, try reading, discussion, creative games, and puzzles. Train in hypnosis under qualified teachers. Creativity training and memory training are all challenging.

If you are eager to be different and creative, then look to new hobbies, from cooking to photography to writing.

A promising area often overlooked as an alternative to drugs, according to Hyde, is service to others.

"Some may be desperate about our social and political situation and try to forget it or rebel against it through the fog of drugs," she says. "The alternatives are not only more constructive but can be very fulfilling on a personal level. In the political area, people can get involved and work for particular candidates or in nonpartisan political projects, as in lobbying for ecological groups. One of the most powerful sets of alternatives, available to almost everyone, consists of getting involved in social service—helping others. This could include: helping the poor; providing companionship to the lonely; helping those in trouble with drugs or family problems; or helping out in voluntary organizations (like the YMCA, Boys Clubs, Big Brothers, Girl Scouts, etc.)."

Service to others has two angles. It not only helps us with our own health, in a negative way, by keeping us out of drug danger, but it contributes to the health of others in society.

HOMESICKNESS

10

Not Tired Enough to Sleep

Shelley slammed the door of the car in the hot grassy parking lot, high above the lake at the Girl Scout camp in central Michigan. `

One whole week with the Girl Scouts!

"Mom! Dad! We go this way," Shelley said, as she hauled up her sleeping bag and a tote bag. She glanced around to make sure they were coming with the extra stuff.

Wooden steps led up to a platform with a cabin that said "D," as her instruction paper indicated. Shelley and her parents left her things there. Then she skipped down the stairs to a nearby group and leader. Shelley looked around to make sure her parents followed.

A young woman in a tennis outfit was putting down names on a clipboard. "You're Shelley. Good. Nice to have you with us."

Shelley told the leader that she had already found her cabin and then waited breathlessly for the first instruction.

"The rest of the kids are down at the water pier, Shelley," the camp leader said.

Shelley got the idea. She could hardly wait to get down there. "Bye, Mom, bye, Dad!"

By nighttime Shelley was tired, but not tired enough to go to sleep. The other kids giggled, even when Shelley was tired of giggling. She missed her favorite pillow. The cabin was musty. It made her want to sneeze. There was no warm hump at the foot of the bed, made by a familiar "Jingo," the cat back home. The sounds were different: instead of an occasional honk, there were croaks, peeps, and, wow, what was that screech? There were no footsteps of Mom or Dad, no distant TV sounds. Croak, peep, screech. Shelley thought about home. It seemed all so far, a whole distant world. Now she was out somewhere in orbit in the woods. So far away. Home. Shelley was homesick.

Have you ever been homesick? If you were, how far were you from home?

Do you think Shelley was really homesick? Or do you think she just thought she was homesick?

Sometimes kids get so homesick they really get sick and have to go home. What will happen to Shelley?

If Shelley's homesickness gets worse, what will she be like the next day? What should the camp counselor do or tell Shelley?

What are good ways to avoid homesickness or get over it?

Sally, ten, of Ambler, Pennsylvania, remembers when she was homesick, and she has some advice. Sally was one of a group of kids at the interfaith Ambler Area Day Camp that met at St. Alphonsus Roman Catholic Church in Maple Glen, Pennsylvania. The camp included Lutheran, Presbyterian, Methodist, Catholic, United Church of Christ groups, and others. Said Sally:

"I get homesick when I am away from my mother for a few days. For example, I went to the shore with my aunt. And I was really looking forward to going because my friend was going to be there too. But the night before I left I got homesick already. I still went. My mother was going to call every other day, and she did. It seemed like after each phone call I got homesick. Usually I only got homesick at night. I was so glad to see my family when I got home."

Sally suggests these five ways to beat the homesickness blues:

1. Think that you will see them again.
2. Imagine what is happening while you're away.
3. Think of how much fun you're having.
4. Think about other things.
5. Cry and get it all out.

Allen, eleven, at the St. Alphonsus Christian Day Camp, overcame the homesickness blues, he says, when he went to New Orleans with his aunt. He was not "overly homesick," he says, because he followed his own suggestions:

1. Prepare yourself before trips. (Plan what you're going to do ahead of time.)
2. Call your family at least once a week.
3. Write letters and postcards.
4. Don't worry.
5. Try not to think of your family too much.

Some of the kids in the St. Alphonsus group said phone calls home were good. Others said, no, they just made you more homesick.

You have to decide what is best for you—whether you should try to forget home, or be reminded of home, or a little bit of both.

Remember, in a place like a camp, you have to think of others, too. A camp counselor can't keep activities rolling if kids insist on calling home all the time.

If you have never really been away from home, and a trip of one week or longer is coming up, tool up for it by inviting a friend over. Then, perhaps, stay at the friend's house. Week-long trips or month-long trips—or all-summer trips—are no more than a series of one-day sleepovers.

"Just take one day at a time," says Bernie Dunphy-Linnartz, national youth leader for the United Presbyterian Church. If you really can't get over the feelings of homesickness, he says, "figure out what it is you miss from home and try to work out a substitute. For instance, if you are used to setting the table around mealtime at home, then why not volunteer to set the table at camp?"

Among the ideas for overcoming homesickness, psychologist Salvatore Didato offers this survival kit for homesickness, originally printed in *Kidbits* (June 1981) magazine:

1. "Before you leave home, prepare yourself mentally. Tell yourself that if the blues come, this time you'll meet and conquer them. Being aware of what's ahead is a good way to reduce the discomfort later on.

2. "It may help to take along some favorite possessions like a small radio, a picture, a baseball glove, a pair of skates.

3. "If you're feeling down, don't hide it. Find someone and tell them a little about how you feel. Chances are, they feel the same way.

4. "Help yourself out of your mood. Don't wait for someone to come over and rescue you. Go where others are.

5. "Focus on friends and topics. When you find someone to talk to, open up to them. Discuss where you're from, your school, hobbies. You'll find that conversation helps to soothe your feelings.

6. "Join any activity if you're invited into it, no matter what you might think about it.

7. "If you spot someone who looks down in the dumps, it's good to try to cheer him or her up. This helping process is a sure-fire technique which will lift your own mood, too.

8. "Give yourself more than the usual amount of satisfactions. They will perk you up. Buy yourself or a friend a soda or snack.

9. "Volunteer for things to do around the camp. It's good to keep busy this way, as well as in the other activities, and, at the same time, be appreciated for it, too.

10. "Don't be a loner. Look forward to making new friends. Remember, strangers at camp are only friends you haven't met."

JEALOUSY

11

"I Saw Him First. He's Mine!"

Fill in the lines of this play.

MANDY: Why are you doing this to me?
JILL:
MANDY: You know what I am talking about!
JILL:
MANDY: Why don't you leave well enough alone?
JILL:
MANDY: I saw him first. I met him first. He's mine!
JILL:
MANDY: Besides, we're just right for each other. He's got nothing in common with you.
JILL:
MANDY: Get off my back.
JILL:
MANDY: Who's jealous?

I suppose you could fill in "Uh-huh," and "huh," and "I dunno" for most of Jill's remarks. It wouldn't make much difference. Mandy was angry, and it was a special kind of anger, jealousy. Jill was stealing her boyfriend.

Boyfriends and girlfriends were on the minds of kids at the Clarksville (Tennessee) Academy when they were asked about jealousy.

Their stories have something in common, at least in the

69

way the jealousy problem seemed to have worked out for
them in the long run.

Jealousy—over a girl—was a real problem for Jerry,
sixteen, who is 6'4", has blue eyes, and likes "high risk
sports"—football, skiing, four wheelin' (Jeep, RV, 4WD)
racing. He says: "As much as I hate to say it, at times I'm a
very jealous type. Mainly when it deals with my girlfriend
(I'm very possessive). One time I took her to a public school
dance. Right when we got in she went straight over to all
her friends from the school, the ones that she only sees
once every two months. I didn't mind her talking to them,
but when half the guys all wanted and got a hug it bothered
me (it was a very affectionate hug). We fought for a couple
of days and finally got over it."

Jealousy over competition for his girl is the problem of
Don, fifteen, who is 205 pounds, a weight lifter, and likes
to repair lawn mowers:

"I was trying to get a girl to go on a date. It was a slow
type of persuasion. Anyhow, things were going great.
Then one day, I came to school and she had another boy's
jacket on. I wasn't really jealous, but very angry. I wish I
could give him a 'cement overcoat' and drop him in the
Hudson. Plus, this little runt was one grade younger than
the girl! I could have crushed his nose, but I didn't. I just
stayed away from her. Later, I thought she was trying to
make me jealous."

Holding on to a boyfriend occupies Mary, sixteen, who
likes basketball and other sports:

"I was dating a guy who went to a local college. Every day
he would tell me he talked to and sat by a girl who was a
few years older than me. I didn't let him know I was jealous
until the situation continued.

"About a week passed, and Jim began to act like nothing
in the world mattered to him except school. This burned
me up and I just knew that he was seeing this girl. She was
blonde, skinny, white (as a ghost), and wore the ugliest nail

polish and lipstick. I worried for a while, and we began to fight about her all of the time. One night he called her to find out what his homework was. Naturally, I felt like going to see her. And I did. She worked at a local store and I just happened to go there. I talked to her and felt like slapping her face. But I held back, and, looking at her, I realized she was nothing special, after all. At that time I told myself to forget about her. I tried but it was always on my mind. I am still dating this guy and am still jealous. But the best thing to do is act like I don't even care."

His best friend got into the act, which troubled Robert, sixteen, who likes sports and cars:

"I had been dating a girl for almost two years and I had never been jealous. Except when my best friend asked her to a dance. We had played basketball, football, and baseball together since seventh grade. He was much bigger than I and he could drive. I was not jealous of him, because he could play sports, because I had started just as many years ago as he and I was a year younger. Why I was jealous was because he could drive and I couldn't. I was jealous of that guy until it was time for the dance. About the time the dance came around, I had my license and a better date to the dance. Now I have my old girlfriend back, and I am not jealous of my friend."

But would Robert's "old girlfriend" be jealous if she knew he said he took a "better date" to the dance?

The helpful thing the teens have in common is "time." In most cases, time was on their side. Jealousy somehow wears down or is forgotten—or at least kept in tow—with the passage of time.

Waiting it out solved the problem for Mark, a fifteen-year-old football player at the same academy:

"In football practice the coach played two people more than he would me, and each of them were worse than I was, and I would sit on the bench in most of practice while they would get to play, and the worst thing was, it was hard for me to get a chance to play. It would not bother me if they were real good, but the only reason I could think of why they were in there was that they played baseball and I didn't, so the coach liked them better. This lasted for most of the season, but the next year I got to play most of the time."

Jealousy is a very natural emotion for a pre-teen or teen to feel in the time of rapid development that young people experience, says Dr. Barry Ginsberg, a school psychologist, in Doylestown, Pennsylvania. "It's hard not to want everything," he says of this period of time. That goes for friends, too. One is protective of what he or she has, including friends. When somebody is taking something away, it is easy to feel jealousy or hatred or envy toward that person.

Edward Podolsky, in his book *The Jealous Child* (Philosophical Library, 1954), says that a person "is jealous when he wants something that someone else has and he has not. This something may be physical, mental, emotional, economic, social, financial, etc. Jealousy, when it is not exaggerated, is normal."

Jealousy is a part of instinct, Podolsky says. An instinct has a purpose. It helps us to survive. Podolsky says:

"Jealousy is an emotion. What is an emotion? Essentially it is a state of intense feeling. An emotion has a definite physiological purpose. It tends to keep the body from losing its equilibrium (balance) during stress. . . . An emotion is a meaningful performance. It is mobilized in certain situations for definite purposes. While experiencing an emotion, we live in another world—in a world where things are pleasanter. This is one of the purposes of an emotion—to save the individual in an unstable situation."

When do your emotions show? Anytime other than when you are jealous?

If emotions serve purposes, are there such things as bad emotions?

When was the time you were most jealous?

Do you remember a time when you were jealous? Does it seem so important now?

The Bible says that God is a "jealous God" (Ex. 20:5). What does that mean?

If it's OK to be jealous sometimes, how much is enough? When is a person "too" jealous?

If you tend to be too jealous, the teens at the Clarksville Academy suggest:

1. "Talk it over with a friend. Ask what he or she would do."

2. "Just try your best to be yourself."

3. "Keep doing your best in whatever you do well."

4. "Try to forget the person—'there are more fish in the sea.' "

5. "Do something to let off the frustration—punch a pillow, lift weights, run a mile."

6. "Put yourself in the other person's shoes."

7. "Think over what you're jealous about. Is being jealous going to help you reach your goal?"

8. "Think about how it affects you. Will you be the loser? Jealousy makes people ugly."

9. "Don't hold it inside."

10. "Get to know the person you are jealous of a little better."

And the teacher of the ninth and tenth grades at the Clarksville Academy, Alice Cortner, suggests: "Try enough objectivity so you can see your own positive points. Then, recognize, don't explain away or rationalize, your jealousies."

12

Elephants Don't Like Dark Rooms

A weary traveler, in medieval times, stopped late one evening at a monastery and asked for food and shelter. He was let in at once and taken to the dining hall.

The abbot in charge apologized for offering only fish and chips, but explained that it was Friday, and Catholics did not eat meat on Friday.

The fish and chips turned out to be the best the traveler had ever eaten. He praised them so highly that the abbot thought it would be good for the chef to be told in person how much his work was liked.

The traveler went to the kitchen and walked toward a man in a big white hat. "Are you the fish fryer?" he asked.

"No," was the reply. "I am the chipmunk."

Speaking of chipmunks, did you ever notice how nervous chipmunks are, always darting this way and that, and, when you think about it, how lonely they are? Did you ever see more than one chipmunk at a time? A chipmunk never seems to attract friends or sit still long enough to get into the thick of things. His is a lonely life.

Some animals appear less lonely. You don't find them off in dark corners by themselves. Elephants, buffalo, elk, deer, lions live in herds. Human beings live in herds or communities, but they can get away by themselves.

Living in groups, for human beings at least, can also be lonely. You can feel alone or lonely in the midst of people.

If nobody is listening to you, or if people are picking on you, you indeed can be lonely among people.

And psychologists point out that you can be very much alone and not be lonely. Being alone and loneliness may be very different. Going to a movie by yourself, or sitting in your room jamming with your favorite record or cassette, or walking a beach all alone looking for shells are all examples of being alone and not necessarily being lonely. Being lonely, or feeling loneliness, is a situation when you are cut off from other people, even in the midst of people, or cut off from things you want to do (you may be bored) and wishing you could relate to another person, or group, or even another thing or hobby.

Dan Carlinsky, writing in *Seventeen* magazine (February 1981), says his talks with psychologists and others show that they seem to think loneliness "is really an inner feeling, a sense that something is missing. Loneliness is wanting more in the way of social relationships; it's being—or feeling—isolated and dissatisfied."

On the other hand, being alone is something we might seek and cherish. Certainly privacy—keeping little brother or sister out of one's room, for example, is something that most kids might want. But loneliness—when you want to be listened to, when you want to be near another person or be a part of a group or happening—is something to be avoided.

There are many who choose to be alone. The "cloistered" monks and nuns who go into monasteries or convents do not come out but stay secluded and give themselves to a life of prayer. Some of these, such as the Trappist monks, do not even talk with one another. This sounds terribly lonely, but they are not lonely, rather alone, as they would put it, with God.

Johann R. Hug, publisher of one of the most widely read children's magazines in Europe, *Junior*, sets off by himself with a donkey and, sometimes, a guide to hike six months at a time by himself, in India, in Italy, and other places. In the 1970s a young woman called the "Camel Woman" hiked alone with four camels and a dog for five months across the 800-mile-wide Gibson Desert of Australia. In history, there were the holy hermits who did everything alone, by choice. The most weird of them was Simeon Stylites, who lived on top of a pillar in Asia Minor for thirty years, until he died.

Perhaps these people were lonely at times, wishing they could be with other people and sharing things, although being alone did not necessarily make them lonely.

Most people are sometimes lonely, researchers say. In a study at the University of Chicago, seventy-five teens were given beepers. When researchers rang the beepers, the teens were to tell how they felt at that moment. When they were alone, the study showed, most of the teens were not unhappy or lonely. They were lonely only when they felt they were missing out on something—for instance, if they ended up alone on a Friday or Saturday night.

> *How much of the time are you alone each week?*
> *What do you like about these times, or not like?*
> *How are these words different—solo, solitude, lonesome, lonely, alone?*
> *When is the last time you felt lonely, either alone or in a group?*
> *In that instance, was there any way to keep from feeling lonely?*

Students at the Summit Hill Junior High School in Frankfort, Illinois, could think of many times they felt lonely:

—"One hot summer day in May, while all my sisters were gone at my grandma's house. I sat on my front doorstep all alone, with nothing to do. All my friends lived in the other part of town, and the ones that did live by me were gone. I went for a short bike ride to the store; after I had gotten done eating, then I took our dog Rufus for a walk around the block. The rest of the day I stayed in and helped my mom clean and make supper."—Boy, 11.

—"I was lonely when my dog died."—Boy, 11.

—"I was very lonely about a week ago when my best friend moved. I didn't have anyone to play with."—Girl, 11.

—"I was lonely when I got in a fight with my best friend."—Boy, 12.

—"I was lonely when I took my friends to McDonald's. My mom went with us and we met some of my mom's friends and one of her friends' daughter, and all my friends sat by them and there wasn't enough room for me so I had to sit at a table by myself."—Girl, 12.

—"I was baby-sitting for the first time, for myself. I was all alone in a big house, but now I like the peace and quiet."—Girl, 12.

—"One time when I was lonely, I didn't do what most teens would do, like blast a radio and let the whole block know that you were home and like a certain song. I just like to sit and maybe read a book, or if something good is on television like *Nova*."—Boy, 12.

—"I was lonely when my girlfriend was out of school for a week straight with strep throat."—Boy, 13.

—"One day my dog ran away. I was very upset, because I would play with her a lot. I felt so helpless like there was nothing I could do to help or find her. We looked, but when we didn't find her, and we could not look anymore, I felt mad because since we did not find her I blamed it on my dad for not looking anymore."—Girl, 13.

—"I spent the night at my friend's. When I got home I found out my parents were getting separated. None of my friends' parents were separated."—Girl, 11.

—"I was lonely when my mother and I would argue, because I would get upset and go into my room. Sometimes it feels like you're not loved, especially when you're close to your mother."—Girl, 12.

—"My friend, David—he always wants to do things that are so dumb, and he does things that I can't do. It is very lonely when a friend of yours is having fun with stuff you don't like."—Boy, 12.

—"My parents were at work as their usual day goes and my sister was at school as she does on a Friday. I was at home in my bedroom. I had a cold and couldn't go out, but it was such a beautiful day and I really felt better. I looked outside and nobody was there, nobody home, nobody at my house, and nobody on the television. My radio was broken and it was silent. I was so lonely."—Girl, 13.

Being lonely at times is a part of being a young person. Some people mistakenly believe that old folks are more lonely. But studies at New York University and the University of California show that old folks are less lonely. That's because their lives are not changing as fast, they feel more independent, and their friendships have been steady for them for years.

Young persons, as they come into new areas of life, get very anxious. Psychologists point out this is true with teens, as they develop interests in the opposite sex. Says Dr. Carin Rubenstein, associate editor of *Psychology Today* magazine, in Leonard Gross's book *The Parents' Guide to Teenagers* (Macmillan, 1981): "Although they may have friends whom they see quite often, many teenagers are desperately looking (often for the first time) for love and romance. Indeed, they usually seek the *perfect* romance, as seen only on television or in the movies. Their frustration in this search, coupled with their gradual separation from parents, may make them feel alone and unloved regardless of how many friends they have. Also, for the first time they are aware that their thoughts are private and not shared by anyone."

We are not going to overcome all our feelings of loneliness. But we can realize that there is very little perfection in life—that people will not always be the way we want them to be, that sometimes our hopes will be shattered, and that sometimes we will be left out of a group, or isolated even in a family setting.

The best way to overcome feelings of loneliness is to own up to the fact that you are lonely and then do something about it.

Kids at the Summit Hill school suggest:

1. "Don't hide."
2. "Be talkative."
3. "Talk to someone on the phone."
4. "Draw or paint something."
5. "Play a game with your parents."
6. "Cook a dinner, or clean the house."
7. "Make a tree house, or plant a garden, ride your bike, bounce a ball."
8. "Tease your brother!"
9. "Watch TV."
10. "Join a club."
11. "Read a book."
12. "Write someone you like."

When you think you are going to be lonely, plan your time, says Larry E. Kalp, secretary for Older Childhood Education of the United Church of Christ. This helps to overcome the "fear of being lonely," which may be worse than being lonely, he says.

Kids used to join clubs and groups, such as the Scouts, more than they do today, Kalp points out. Clubs do help, if you belong. But most important, plan ahead. Plan to be someplace or to do something, whether with somebody or alone. You can learn to be alone and enjoy it, but don't settle for loneliness.

13

Nobody Is Better than Me

Cathy, thirteen, lives just outside Clarksville, Tennessee, near the Kentucky border, and attends the Clarksville Academy. She likes to play basketball and the piano, but sometimes she doesn't feel very important. At times she has (as most people have) what is called low esteem. For Cathy, it's like this:

"When I go to choir on Wednesday night, I feel like I'm nobody. Nobody from my school that's my age goes except for a girl I don't get along with most of the time. There are a whole lot of people from public schools, but none of them talk to me, even if I try and talk to them. I'm not that good at making new friends or meeting people. I'm kind of shy and people can't understand what I say most of the time, because I don't talk very loud, and I can't help it. I've never been able to talk loud. So everybody ignoring me at church on Wednesdays makes me feel like I'm not important at all. I have some friends at church, but they don't come on Wednesdays."

Says Diane, thirteen, Cathy's classmate, of a time she felt as if she wasn't worth much:

"Well, we were at Bradon Springs. A boy that I liked and loved asked a girl to go with him. But she was not a nice girl at all. But he saw something in her. She told me that she would not go with him because she liked me. But what did she do? She went with him. I cried two nights on this. I could have killed them both. Today she broke up with him, but she says it was just to see how he will act. He is taking it hard. I do feel sorrow for him. I still love him and I am sure that I always will. He is so cute."

Many teens have a low regard of themselves when they fail or do something wrong, but David, twelve, who is in the same class as the two girls mentioned above, felt worthless when he succeeded at being bright. It's how he handled himself. He recalls:

"I was in science, our teacher was asking us questions. I got every one right. She said, quote, 'You're doing well, aren't you, David?' I raised my hands, clapping. After that I thought about what I just did. I realized that I was acting like one of the most snobbish people I had ever seen. I felt very bad."

Have you ever held yourself in low esteem? Why?

How do you feel when you have low regard for yourself?

Do you usually have a high esteem of yourself? Why, or why not?

Whose fault is it when a person has low esteem of himself or herself?

Is there a difference between holding yourself in low esteem and feeling guilty?

Here are some other reasons why kids hold themselves in low esteem. These come from Noel Leeney's Academy class and from Linda Ennis' fifth-grade class at the Thomas Richards School, Atco, New Jersey. They feel low esteem when:

—"People make fun of my name."

—"You know you are right, then somebody who doesn't know as much proves you're wrong."

—"I got an F in science, and I knew when I got home I would get it."

—"A boy said he didn't like me."

—"I was playing a prank and I didn't mean to, but I hurt him."

—"My dog got stolen. He was the best trained beagle."

—"I was catching for my baseball team, when a kid stole second, and I made a bad throw, and he went to third."

—"I tried out for the all stars and didn't make it."

—"We got killed in a kickball game."

—"I wanted to be in acting club and didn't make it."

—"I lost a wrestling match."

—"I lost a friend."

—"My parents separated."

—"I raised my hand to do something in class. I never get picked."

To think more highly of yourself, as one boy, twelve, at the school in Atco, New Jersey, put it, you should do just that: "I would say if you think highly of yourself, then other people will think highly of you."

Another, a girl of eleven, in the same school, urged kids not to judge themselves by others. She said: "Most people who don't do well in school try to act 'cool,' so they don't look like fools. If they just tried, they might find out they like it and they might enjoy themselves more. Always be yourself, because you are more important than the kid that you copy off of."

Both the Atco and the Clarksville kids say, "Try harder" and "help others." Doing both at least keeps one from having feelings of self-pity, for low esteem involves a certain amount of feeling sorry for oneself.

Says Joe, thirteen, at the Clarksville Academy: "Something I always like to say when I lose a girlfriend. If you love something, set it free. If it comes back, it's yours, if it doesn't, it never was! I like this. It helps me realize that I can't let one person get me down. You just have to forget it."

Since life is always changing, kids whose lives change fast need to sit back once in a while and ask a few questions, especially if there is a problem, says Dr. Tony Meade of the Institute for Juvenile Research in Chicago.

Dr. Meade talks of "age appropriateness." He means there are certain things we should do at certain ages, and sometimes kids are holding back or getting too far ahead of the "appropriate" age level. One may be tiny for his or her age, or too big. Taunts like "Hi, Runt" or "Hey, Godzilla" may just have to be taken in stride. Most are going to catch up or level off with the others at some point. And of course, he says, there is a kind of balancing act: a young person who has a problem can seek achievement and attention in another area, such as sports or good school marks.

Kids should strive to be in their "appropriate age" of activities. "Playing with little lead army men is appropriate at one age, but not at others," says Dr. Meade.

Nobody has to hold himself or herself in low esteem, says a man who prepares materials for the classroom. Dr. Herbert R. Adams, who has a doctor's degree in education from Harvard and is director of the Secondary School Division of Science Research Associates in Chicago, says: "If a kid holds himself in low esteem, tell him to look at what a miracle he is. Pick up a pencil and have him hold it between his forefinger and thumb. That's a miracle.

"Or, look at a tiny grain of salt and the wonder of it. Every individual also is miraculous. The problem is people grow up not knowing the miracle they are or do not accept it. Take responsibility for yourself. Start with yourself as perfect."

MONEY

14

"All I Want for Christmas Is Cash"

They came from far away, kings and prime ministers, the Vice-President of the United States and the wife of the President (Mrs. Nixon), and important people of all kinds.

They moved into expensive tents, draped in red velvet and furnished with Persian carpets.

They were the guests at a national birthday party thrown by the late shah of Iran, Mohammed Riza Pahlavi, at a cost of $11 million, at the site of the ancient ruins of Persepolis. The Shah's queen wore what one reporter described as buckets of emeralds, as many as she could bear. The guests dined sumptuously on quail eggs stuffed with caviar, lamb and peacock, and the finest liquor in the world.

For the birthday, which marked the twenty-five hundredth anniversary of the founding of the Persian Empire by Cyrus the Great, roads were cordoned off, buildings whitewashed along the way, and even some walls were put up so the wealthy visitors would not be able to see the poverty along the roadside.

Whether the Shah did some good, building new roads, hotels, generating plants, and other projects with his money was still being debated at the time of his death in 1981, as the people of his nation, now in ruins, clamored for his life.

But Persepolis and the big bash there is the story of great

wealth spent on the wealthy, while the poor were needy and hungry.

Then, there is the other kind of story, in contrast to that of the Shah. Young John Wesley, in the eighteenth century, at Oxford University in England, founded the Methodists. Wesley and his young friends were so orderly and well organized that other students made fun of them and called them "Methodists," too methodical.

Unlike the latter-day Shah—and other shahs and kings, Wesley lived as simply as possible. He probably was not a very interesting man, but he could spellbind a crowd when he spoke to poor coal miners and factory workers in the countryside of England.

Wesley had some strong and different views about money. Here's his motto: "Having *gained,* in a right sense, *all you can,* and *saved all you can:* in spite of nature, and custom, and world prudence, *give all you can*" (*Arminian Magazine,* 1781).

Wesley told the story of a young man (perhaps himself) who received 30 pounds in English currency in his first year at work and found that he needed 28 to live on. So the young man gave away the other two. "The next year, receiving 60 pounds, he still lived on 28, and gave away two and 30. The third year he received 90 pounds, and gave away 62. The fourth year he received 120 pounds. Still he lived as before on 28; and gave the poor 92. Was not his a more excellent way?"

Which of these people do you like best? The Shah or the man in Wesley's story? Why?

What do the stories tell us about happiness? Which person deep inside was possibly happiest? Why?

Would you like to be like either the Shah or Wesley? Is there another kind of person whose use of money you admire?

What would happen if you combined the views of the Shah and Wesley? Would that work—spending wildly one time and being tightfisted another? Or would there be something wrong with that approach to money?

Is money good or bad?

Young people from several schools answered that last question:

At the Benton Consolidated High School in Benton, Illinois, and the Clarksville Academy in Clarksville, Tennessee, they were divided on whether money is good or bad. Money is good, bad, and "in between."

Money is good because:
—"You need money to buy things."
—"It lets you do a lot of things you can't do without it."
—"Where would we be without it?"
—"Without it you would probably die."
—"It's entertainment."
—"It allows people to work to get material things in life that make life happier."
—"Without it the world would be in confusion."

Money is bad because:
—"You always want more than you have."
—"Money has made taxes, high prices and a lot of troubles. Although money can buy food, cars, and lots of other stuff, money can't buy your feelings, like love can."
—"It causes wars."
—"If you aren't careful, it takes over."

Money is both good and bad because:
—"It's good for buying cars and presents and things, but it causes bad things like bank robberies."
—"It's OK just as long as it doesn't become an obsession with you."
—"It does tend to make people evil and overpowering and it also can help people."
—"Money is good when you can have most of the things

you want and need. It can be bad when you let it control your life."

Money does buy the groceries and pay the bills. But money can be much more, depending on what's important to you. How you spend your money will tell a lot about your personality, your friends, your goals—or problems you have with your personality, friends, or goals or lack of goals.

If money becomes everything, then you are heavy into materialism, gaining the new material things that come along. The things that money buys become all that counts.

"We have a real problem with the dollar sign in our society," says Irma Stahl, teen program consultant for the National Board of the YWCA, New York. "A lot of teens are into name brands, designer jeans, for instance." To her, the "keeping up" in possessions and clothes is materialism.

And she says society encourages young people to build their lives around money and getting it. One example, she says, is going after jobs just because they pay well and not because one feels good about them. Money becomes the really big thing.

With some kids, money seems to be the only thing that counts. Have you ever heard someone say, or said yourself to an uncle or aunt or other relative: "Just give me money for Christmas!"

Young people at the Clarksville, Tennessee, and Benton, Illinois, schools were asked what they thought about "Don't give me a gift for Christmas (or birthday). Give me money!"

The Clarksville kids said:

—"I think it doesn't matter what you get. It's the thought that counts."—Boy, 9.

—"I think to give money is very cruel. A gift is better than nothing."—Boy, 11.

—"I think it's good for a birthday but not for Christmas."—Boy, 11.

—"It's rude to give money."—Girl, 11.

—"It's not right to give money. A gift, you can keep forever."—Girl, 10.

—"I think you should appreciate what you are getting and don't be picky."—Girl, 11.

—"I think you take what you get and if they give you money, use it wisely."—Girl, 10.

The Benton teens added:

—"Sometimes I would like to have money instead of a gift. There may be something I want to buy. I would rather have something I like than a gift I didn't want."—Girl, 16.

—"It's nice to get gifts, but money is better."—Boy, 16.

—"I don't think I would like money. I would rather get a gift. I feel it is much more personal and means more. Also with money I would be more apt to waste it."—Girl, 15.

—"You would lose the sentimental value, but you don't have the problem of getting something you don't want."—Boy, 16.

—"I think if a person says this, he shouldn't get either one. If he is picky about what he gets, he shouldn't get anything."—Boy, 16.

—"I think you should let the person who is giving the gift decide. If they choose to give you money, fine. But let them decide."—Girl, 15.

—"I don't like getting money. Because if I get money for Christmas or my birthday, I would end up spending it on something stupid like food or candy."—Girl, 15.

—"I would rather have a gift. Because a gift is more cherishing than money."—Boy, 16.

—"Money is OK. If you get a present you don't like, it will just sit there."—Boy, 16.

—"When someone says they want money, they usually really mean they want a gift."—Boy, 15.

—"I think giving money is a cover-up; then usually this person will be stingy."—Boy, 15.

—"I think if someone told me that (he or she wanted money), I wouldn't give them the time of day."—Boy, 15.

—"I think it is easier to give money but you should take what you get and not be a snot about it."—Girl, 15.

—"I would like to have half and half."—Boy, 15.

How many of the kids and teens above do you feel you know pretty well from what they say about gifts—and money?

15

Creatures Next Door, Below, or Above

"Our neighbor really isn't much fun to live next to," says Beth, thirteen, of the North Junior High School in St. Cloud, Minnesota.

"They have two dogs that keep us up all night long, and they play baseball right by our windows very early in the morning."

Charlene, also thirteen, in the same school, has some neighbors that "are not very nice at all. They come home late and they have been drinking. They get really loud and don't realize that the neighbors might be asleep. Also, the kids are not nice at all. When other neighbor kids go outside to play, those kids have to go bother them and not be nice at all."

Other kids tell of neighbors who borrow everything; neighbors with loud stereos; neighbors who throw things in the yard; neighbor kids who break things or pull up flowers and so on. Some even have neighbors that won't speak to them and neighbors they never see, and so they are not much fun to live next door to either.

Few neighbors are as bad as Dan Akroyd in the movie *The Neighbors,* in which cars and houses were destroyed in the escalating war with neighbor John Belushi.

What do you do when you have bad neighbors?
What is a good neighbor?

Can a neighbor be too good?
What's the neighbor you like the most? Why?
Are you a pretty good neighbor? Or a bad neighbor? What makes you think so?

Sometimes if neighbors are bad, you might ask why or how they got that way.

A youngster who is vandalizing the neighborhood may just want attention, according to Chicago psychologist Robert Nicolay. "Vandalism is the most primitive contact," he says. "A kid doing it is expressing a need to contact other people and can't."

And Dr. Nicolay says that most kids get attitudes about neighbors from their parents. But he suggests that if your parents don't like a neighbor, you should ask yourself if your parents are right about the neighbor.

If kids are all over your property or yard, it might help to realize that kids do not always understand the idea of property as adults do. "They are idealistic and are not aware of artificial barriers," says Irma Stahl, teen program consultant for the National Board of the YWCA.

She says that if there is something bad or disagreeable with your neighbor, it doesn't mean you have to be on bad terms. "If the dog barks, it's not personal. They are not out to persecute you."

She suggests offering to help with the yard or in some other way as a means of getting along with a neighbor. Problems can be faced a lot better if you are friends.

One man in Atlanta, Georgia, tells how he got his "bad" neighbors to change a bit. Charles Duncan and his wife shared a building, a duplex, with another family. "The apartment neighbors had a beer bash nearly every Saturday night," said Duncan, executive director of the Georgia Baptist Foundation. "Since I had two preaching engagements each Sunday, I did not need to lose sleep because of their excessive noise." And, "Another next-door neighbor was an alcoholic and abused his wife by both word and deed."

How did he solve his problems? "My wife became friendly with the wife in the other duplex, since they were both at home all day and could not ignore each other, and things got better. I tried to be nice to the alcoholic, and his drinking became less of a problem the longer I knew him.

"Don't fight them. Unless you have an alternative to living near disagreeable neighbors! Friendliness and a genuine concern for the obnoxious person is more likely to make proximity bearable. There is nothing wrong with registering the fact that actions (unreasonable ones) are distracting, but hostility will more often rupture relations so that they are irreparable."

And Mr. Duncan told of a friend who also made the treat-your-enemies-nicely approach work. "Mr. A lived next door to Mr. B, who was an unsavory character and tried to annoy the A family. He was highly successful. The A's had no choice but to ignore much of the intended harassment and endure some of it. Mr. A made an effort to be friendly and started doing business with his neighbor (a dry cleaner). Mr. A and his family moved away after some years. The B's love to have them visit."

The "help them"—friend or enemy—approach worked for Cula Mae Nickum, of Bethlehem, Pennsylvania. She had a neighbor years ago who didn't speak to her, but then "one day she went away and she had wash on her line and it looked like rain. I took her wash off the line and we became friends again."

A construction worker from Boise, Idaho, reports on some neighbors that most of us would like to do without: "The parents are the most obnoxious people. Their horses were always loose. The kids running around. They never gave a damn. They lived in filth. The mother was half crazy anyway. . . . We had the kids over and they liked to help us in the garden, but their parents got mad." This fellow doesn't say how the story ended. Where special problems are involved, maybe there aren't any ready solutions. But, perhaps there would be something to the suggestion that this man and his wife share some of the produce of the garden with the strange, madhouse neighbors, and maybe (and maybe not) the produce could serve as a peace offering.

The kids from North Junior High in St. Cloud, Minnesota, tell what it takes to be a good neighbor:

1. "Keep any pets or other things out of each other's lawns."
2. "If they are gone or on vacation, you could watch their house and yard."
3. "Let each other borrow things."
4. "Help your neighbor out whenever they need it."
5. "Always be nice and smile."
6. "Respect your neighbor's privacy."
7. "Include them when you're doing things."
8. "Don't be disrespectful."
9. "Be considerate of their property."
10. "Visit once in a while."

In crowded areas and big-city ghettos, the problems of neighbors rank very low, according to James Cone of Union Theological Seminary in New York. The question of dogs and the like are not the problem; the problem is survival. Still, people have to relate and work together anywhere in order to have a livable community. "Find what you can do to eliminate the problems of the ghetto (or neighborhood)," says Dr. Cone. "Find a common task of service in which you and your neighbors can work."

16

Worming Into the Wallpaper

"I was so shy that whenever company came over to my house I would go to my room and I'd remain there until all the guests were gone. And whenever I saw kids playing or having a good time outside, I'd wish I wasn't so shy, because I wanted to join them. But somehow I never did join them."

So says Dorothy, a sixteen-year-old girl from William Penn High School in Philadelphia, remembering just how shy she really was.

But that's not all of her story. "Well," she says, "I got over shyness by being around people who aren't shy." But getting over shyness, she says, takes a little time. "I'd say, don't force yourself to stop being shy. Let it come naturally. That's what I did.

"It was very hard for me to adjust myself from being shy to being open with everyone. But seriously though, I still have just a bit of shyness within me."

And so does most everybody else. It's a universal experience, says Philip G. Zimbardo in his book *Shyness: What It Is—What to Do About It* (Addison-Wesley, 1977). According to Dr. Zimbardo, professor of social psychology at Stanford University, his research at the Stanford Shyness Clinic shows more than 80 percent of those questioned were shy at some point in their lives. Forty percent said they were currently shy. To Dr. Zimbardo, that means four out of ten

Americans are shy, some 84 million people.

Everybody knows what shyness is. You're afraid to speak up, afraid to be around people, and you have a lack of self-confidence.

Lack of self-confidence and shyness may not be the same. An insecure person lacking self-confidence could be an extrovert, that is, forging to the front of every situation. But shyness is associated with quietness, too much quiet, and withdrawing into the background, almost into the wallpaper.

How would you describe the shyest person you know?
Are you like that person in any way?
Think of a time you were shy. Would you be shy today in the same situation? Why or why not?
What is the difference between shyness and humility?
In an election for either a school or public office, you have a choice between a shy candidate and one who is an extrovert, or very forward and outspoken. Who would you vote for and why?

The young people at Dorothy's high school, when asked for examples of shy people they knew, described shy people as:

—Unnoticed in a room
—Nervous around a group of people
—Not willing to trust people
—Slow to start conversations

Students at the Chippewa Hills Junior High School in Barryton, Michigan, see shy persons the same way. Here is a typical description of a shy person, as a Barryton sopho- more girl put it: "My friend is very shy. She always runs from people or just looks at them when they ask a question. I don't even think she talks to her parents a lot. She only talks when she has to."

Students agree that most shy people have good qualities, but that they don't let people see these qualities. There are some exceptions—the shy person who clearly excels, but acts low key. Said a Chippewa High girl, fourteen, of a boy in her class: "He is very shy. He's very quiet, but a good grade student. He gets mostly all A's. He pays more attention to the teachers than the students goofing off in class."

Characteristic of the shy student is a difficulty in speaking up when he or she should. One shy teen at Senn High School in Chicago took a grade lower in nearly all his classes because he was too shy to give the answers when he knew them. Teachers took his lack of response as lack of interest and more often than not as a lack of understanding. Only his good grades on tests rescued him from wiping out in the classes.

Shyness is one of those things that most people in time can work out of or at least control. It is something that people have learned, and so in most normal cases, it is something that can be unlearned. According to Dr. Zimbardo, behavioral scientists say that shyness may be the result of (1) a history of bad or negative experiences with people in certain situations, (2) not learning the "right" social skills, such as manners, ways of speaking, etc., (3) expecting to perform inadequately and therefore becoming constantly anxious about your performance, and (4) learning to put yourself down for your own "inadequacy"—"I am shy," "I am unworthy," "I can't do it," "I need Mommy!"

To overcome shyness, which is really a habit of giving a low-level response or none at all, one has to want to do it. J.B. at William Penn High did what he could to get Jason out of his shyness, but he didn't get much help from Jason, who remained shy: "All the girls in our junior high school thought Jason was a very nice-looking young man. Every time I found two girls for Jason and me to talk to, he would never say much. He would sit and smile for the most part. I thought maybe it was the girls I was introducing him to. But every time I introduced him to a girl, a week later she would be telling me how young he acts. And then there were those same three words that I repeated to everyone, 'He's just shy.' "

J.B. insists that he was once shy himself. "If you knew how I adore females and have to talk to them," he says, "now then you would say, 'He was once shy? Ha, ha, ha!' "

His advice to overcome shyness: "Let loose. Say what's on your mind. And let people know how you feel. Shyness is like a cold. Once it's out of you, you feel much better. Talking to people and speaking to strangers can help you overcome your shyness."

A lot of shyness comes with boy meeting girl, girl meeting boy. In the Kidsday column of the *Cleveland Plain Dealer* newspaper (July 12, 1981), there was advice for a shy boy who wanted to meet a girl:

Dear Kidsday:

I am 12 years old and in sixth grade. I have a problem with my girlfriend. Her name is Becky, and she's very pretty. She likes to do things like go roller-skating and see movies. I'm kind of shy and don't know how to ask her to go places or do things. Can I have some advice?

The Shy Boy

Dear Shy Boy:

We think you are old enough to go on certain kinds of dates with girls. Sometimes it's easier, though, if you go with a bunch of friends. Write Becky a letter and ask her to go roller-skating with you and some other kids. If you are too shy to give the note to her yourself, have a friend do it. Or put it into the mailbox at her house. (But don't be too shy to sign your own name.) If you go with a group, you can have other people around but spend most of your time with Becky. After awhile, maybe you'll feel confident enough to ask her to go roller-skating some Saturday afternoon, just with you.

Dr. Zimbardo suggests making up a chart in which you list times you were shy in one column, then in another column the value of being shy for each instance, and the cost to you in terms of missed opportunities because you were shy in each instance.

Dr. Zimbardo gives "Fifteen Steps to a More Confident You." In summary, they are:

Recognize your strengths, decide what you believe in, discover your roots, do not give in to guilt, look for causes of your action outside yourself, realize there is more than one way of looking at things, never say bad things about yourself, don't let people criticize you as a person (only your actions), remember failure can turn into a blessing sometimes, do not put up with people and situations that make you feel inadequate, find time to relax, practice being sociable, don't overprotect your ego (better to let it get hurt than to play it too cool), set up long-range goals in life, and realize that you are unique. "With confidence in yourself, obstacles turn into challenges and challenges into accomplishments. Shyness then recedes, because, instead of always preparing for and worrying about how you will live your life, you forget yourself as you become absorbed in the living of it."

Being shy, of course, is not necessarily bad. It's what you do with shyness. Dr. Robert Nicolay says: "It's good to be shy. Most people like shy people. Shyness has an appeal. But a shy person has to learn when to move and move at the right times. I had a girl in a book study group who always sat back. Only once in a while would she speak. She would wait, then say, 'I wonder if . . . ,' and then she would say just the right thing, and people listened to her."

A generation ago Enid Haupt wrote a chapter on "Breaking Through the Shyness Barrier" in *The Seventeen*

Book of Young Living (McKay, 1957). Her advice is still helpful.

—Slow down and breathe easily when you enter a crowded room, when you are in any new situation.

—Be sure you stand erectly with your head up—you'll look assured, even if you're not!

—If you have bought new clothes for the occasion, wear the entire outfit at least once beforehand.

—For any new situation, dress simply and carry as few things as possible.

—Move slowly enough so your clothes won't catch on tables or doors or sweep things off low tables.

—Look serene by being still—no twisting a lock of hair, turning a bracelet or ring, twirling a scarf.

—When you are eating, take small bites, chew slowly; first rest your hand on the implement or glass instead of grabbing it up. Take a sip of water before speaking.

—When you're not sure what is expected of you in a new situation, look around the room and take your cue from the others—and don't hesitate to ask someone near you. Asking someone to help you is a good way to start a conversation and perhaps to make a new friend. (You remember the old joke about everybody loving to give advice and nobody wanting to take it.)

Some people never overcome their shyness, but learn to live with it. Some even go on to become famous. That was the case with George Lucas, producer of *Star Wars, The Empire Strikes Back, Raiders of the Lost Ark,* and other movies. He still felt shy when he returned to his twenty-year high school class reunion in Modesto, California.

An interesting, even amusing account of that reunion with shy George present is recounted by Mark A. Stein, of the *Los Angeles Times* (June 30, 1982):

Lucas himself was remembered as a shy, slight teen-ager who kept to himself, raced a little white Fiat and read comic books constantly.

"He was a real shy kid—short, skinny and big ears," (Steve) Hendley said.

"Everyone talks about George now, of course, but frankly, back then he was just a shadow," said Dennis Kamstra, Lucas' old locker partner.

"You'd never have thought that little George would ever do anything," said Karlene Duckert.

His anonymity was apparent when he and his wife, film editor Marcia Lucas, first arrived at the balloon-festooned hall.

"Ooo! Ooo! There he is!" gushed one classmate as Lucas and his wife began to make their way through the crowd.

"Which one is he?" asked another classmate standing nearby.

"I'm not sure," the first woman replied, "but I'm going to tell him how much I loved my character in the movie."

Given away by his name tag, which bore his high school yearbook photo, Lucas soon began to leave a wake of turned heads as he moved around the room. After a few minutes, people throughout the hall were pointing him out to their friends and queuing up to say hello.

The filmmaker, who still has a reputation for shyness, graciously signed autographs, joshed with his classmates and spoke with reporters throughout the evening. . . .

After dinner, Lucas was not surprisingly a little un-comfortable with all the attention afforded him.

"I don't think anyone wants to come to these things as the 'class loser' or the 'class winner,' " he said. "It's a lot more fun to be one of the crowd in the middle. Then you can just meet friends and talk." (© 1982, *Los Angeles Times*)

He's still shy George, but he gets by.

17

Down a Different Road

Janet's parents had been screaming at each other for several months. Janet usually stayed out of it. But sometimes she would scream back. Her little brother Mitchell usually sat dumbfounded through all the commotion.

Still, Janet was not ready for that Saturday morning, when she started down the steps. Dad had expected to be packed up and out before anybody noticed. He would tell them all that he was leaving only after the car was loaded.

Mom immediately knew what was going on; she had gotten out of bed early.

"So this is it!" Mom shouted, her hands on her hips.

Janet settled midway on the stairs. Numbed, she didn't say anything for a moment. Then she screamed at her dad; when her mother turned to her, she screamed at her. Mitchell soon assembled himself on the stairs, too, and watched dumbfounded.

Janet settled back and watched her father make a few more trips to get things. Tears formed a warm stream on her face, and a glance told her that tears were ebbing down Mitchell's face, too.

Janet had a sense of being at a funeral. Watching the death of one parent. In fact, there was a death—the death of a relationship. And Janet and Mitchell could only mourn as her parents separated.

Her feelings would grow into anger—a sense of betrayal

by her parents, guilt that she helped to cause the separation some way, and a feeling of worthlessness, her world
shattered around her. And above all, there was a fear—a
deep dread of the future. Would she see her dad again?
Will either parent ever love her again? Would she and
Mitchell and Mom be able to stay in the house, would they
move and friends be lost, how would the bills and member-
ships and subscriptions and movies and clothes be paid for
in the future?

Concern over how children in single-parent homes
might fare with the basic needs of life is high among the list
of problems kids associate with divorce.

Fifth-graders in Suzan Young Bramley's class in the
Buckingham (Pennsylvania) Elementary School almost
unanimously suggested that raising money was one of the
big new problems of a separated home. Said one eleven-
year-old: "One of my friends' parents is divorced and it's
hard for her mother to raise the money to support them."

Said another: "A single-parent house might have trouble
feeding children because they might not get enough money."

And not having enough money means the single parent
with whom the kids are living may have to work and that
could lead to neglect. "There might not be enough money
to pay the bills, so the parent that you live with will always
be at work and might not have enough time for you."

Other concerns: "If your parents are divorced, you will
have to go back and forth a lot."

"It will be harder getting places."

"You could be upset because you don't see the other
parent."

"If two people were divorced and one got married, the
child or children might not know which mother to go to
with problems."

Homes broken up by death or divorce do change the
roles of all. One Buckingham fifth-grader was very aware

of this: "When Mary was five, her father walked out on her mother. Now she is nine, and her mother doesn't have a good-paying job. Her family has problems, but they make it through. She has a little sister to take care of. She has been in five different schools. I think she is the best friend I ever had."

Some of you reading this live in a single-parent home. At least six million Americans between the ages of ten and eighteen live with only one parent. About one out of five kids lives with a single parent. A 1982 Gallup Youth Survey found that 32 percent of the teens in the country have experienced the breakup of their parents' marriage.

One out of every two marriages now ends in divorce. So it is possible that half of the babies now being born will be in a home with only the father or the mother as a part of their lives.

Why do parents break up?

Could breakups be avoided if parents tried harder?

What advice would you give kids in a single-parent home?

Should divorced parents remarry?

What advice do you have for quarreling parents?

Is there something missing in single-parent homes?

Can anything good come out of a tragedy, such as a failed marriage?

What useful ideas or rules could you keep in mind, if you are in a single-parent home?

Suzan Bramley, whose fifth-graders discussed divorce and separated homes, explains some of the reasons for the separation of parents: "The world and everything in it is moving at such a rapid pace that it causes some people to change in order to adapt. When changes occur between two married people, it often causes them to change their feelings for one another. It doesn't mean they are bad people, or unloving people, or unfeeling people; and it certainly doesn't mean that the parents have stopped loving them (the child or children). Knowing that parents are human and make mistakes, I would advise them that if they can learn from their parents' mistakes, *there* is the good from the whole experience."

Good can come out of a tragic experience. Ever watch some of those old western movies or TV series where kids had to struggle under adversity—out on the prairie where the weather, greedy land grabbers, disease, death, and all kinds of problems seemed to make the kids stronger for having faced them? Something of that is true as you weather a crisis; you may become a stronger person.

The point of finding strength through difficulty is also made by Dianna Daniels Booher, who has a chapter in her book *Coping: When Your Family Falls Apart* (Messner, 1979), on "Turning the Bad Into the Good."

She asks: "Pain. Have you ever experienced intense physical pain? Had major surgery? Had to exercise a bad knee? If you have, then you know that pain is bearable when it is suffered in the interest of improving your condition—you'll be sick no longer. So, in effect, pain can sometimes bring health.

"So it is with the pain of divorce. Maybe your home situation was very sick, very unhappy—if not for you, at least for your parents. The pain of divorce hurts deeply, but, in the end, healing can come."

Among the possible benefits of the pain of going through a breakup of your parents, she suggests there might come:

1. Relief from a charged home atmosphere. The daily conflicts and explosions of anger might be gone.

2. An improved relationship with your parents. It may mean more time with Dad and/or Mom, as each makes an effort to spend time with you.

3. Better communication. "Both parents and kids need

each other during this time, and they tend to reach out to each other with stronger motivation. It can mean some very close sharing times. . . . And better communication often brings a chance for you to have more say in decisions which affect the home and you."

4. Preparation for the future. Many kids say their parents' divorce has helped them make a better marriage of their own. For one thing, divorce helps kids see marriage for the serious commitment it is. After seeing the pain a bad marriage can bring, they become determined not to enter a marriage lightly.

Sometimes parents improve, Booher points out, by paying more attention to their appearance, sometimes by even going back to school.

During the whole process of a home breakup, from the first shocking announcement to the settling down, months or years later, it is important for kids to be talkative and not to hold in questions or resentments.

"Get answers to all your questions," says Tony Meade of the Institute for Juvenile Research in Chicago. "Face up and ask questions. They (parents) owe you answers. Even make a list. But try to get information: 'How are you going to be my father?' 'When will I see you?' and things like that."

At the same time, allow your parents and your brothers and sisters to have their own feelings. Don't try to impose your outlook on others. "Keep in mind that others' feelings are theirs," says Judi Marks in "The Ups and Downs of Living with a Single Parent," in *Teen Magazine* (July 1982). "By trying to take charge of them, deny them or smooth them over, you're trespassing on someone else's emotional territory."

This applies to getting along with stepparents. While most kids are uneasy, if not outright hostile about mother or dad remarrying and gaining a stepparent who might not understand them, they need to remember that stepparents are humans, too, and they have rights.

If you and your family members go through the heartache process of a family breakup, try to think of others. For instance, if you have a younger brother or sister, you might go to the library and pick up one of the many books that deal with problems and concerns of kids at all ages. Ask your librarian. She or he might look in a book called *Helping Children Cope: Mastering Stress Through Books and Stories,* by Joan Fassler (The Free Press, 1978). This book lists books for kids going through new experiences, including home breakup, moving, and others. For the very young, books suggested include the stories about bears and rabbits and other likable forest friends. You can get these books and read these stories to your brother or sister. In helping him or her over the crisis at home, you may find you are helping yourself.

In the book *My Friend Has Four Parents,* by Margaret O. Hyde (McGraw-Hill, 1981), there is a list of places where parents and kids can get help during a time of home tension and breakup. Some of these places are:

Children of Divorce, Box 122, State College, PA 16801.

Divorced Kids Group, Guidance Center, Lexington High School, Lexington, MA 02173.

Kids in the Middle, 8029 Forsyth Blvd., Clayton, MO 63105.

In your city or area there are the schools, the churches and synagogues, Parents Without Partners, the YMCA and YWCA, and a family or youth service division of your city or county.

STRESS

18

Breathe Through Holes in Your Feet

They are learning to breathe through the holes in their feet.

In one school at least, the Lincoln Junior High School in Skokie, Illinois, kids are taught to deal with the stress in their lives.

Stress is the pressure or strain or heaviness one feels when one is up against a difficult problem, person, or situation.

The holes in the feet are imaginary. But if you lie down and relax and think about your feet—pretending there are holes in them and that you are breathing through those holes—you have one of the ways by which kids at the Lincoln Junior High are told to fight stress.

As the kids think about their feet and take deep breaths, the cool air fills their lungs. The problems get lighter—at least for a while.

There are other techniques that the unusual class at the Lincoln school is using to get at stress. One technique is role-playing—setting up make-believe problem situations, acting out roles, and dealing with the problems.

"People don't think about kids having problems," says Antoinette Saunders, a psychologist who set up the eight-week experimental course for eighth-graders in the school in the Chicago suburb.

"We think of kids as carefree and playful," she said. But

107

kids, she pointed out, worry just as do busy, pressured executives. "We have children with ulcers, backaches, and migraine headaches" (*Philadelphia Inquirer*, April 8, 1982, AP).

Dr. Joyce Brothers, writing in her column in the *Chicago Tribune*, June 3, 1982, says: "Children can suffer from stress just as much, if not more than adults. Unfortunately, they don't have the coping mechanisms adults have. Children can't curse at their parents, slam doors, or fight back. Such behavior isn't tolerated in most homes."

For some kids, stress is akin to a kind of fear or terror. Dr. Robert M. Krauss, chairman of the psychology department at Columbia University in New York says: "They can let the little things get to them, and the prospect of returning a book overdue to the library can be a thing of terror. They have some of the worst kind of stress. They can be told to confront each stressful situation and deal with it. The problem is the more we defer dealing with it, the greater it looms—nothing is as potent as our ability to fantasize. In facing the source of stress, we strip away the self-generated fearsomeness and the monsters go away."

Some problems under different names are just old-fashioned stress. Dr. Charles L. Bassman, an educator and clinical psychologist of Marlton, New Jersey, says that perhaps 7 percent of the kids who are hyperactive are merely reacting under stress.

The roots of many ailments, both bodily and mental, he says, may be traced back to stress, the pressure to do something. Among them are headaches, bowel problems, behavior problems, failing at school, not having friends, and avoiding classmates.

Stress really begins to hit about the sixth or seventh grade, as more change in life comes. "The second to the sixth grade are the best adjusted years in a person's life," says Dr. Robert Nicolay. By the sixth, there are new roles, new schools, new responsibilities, glimpses of adult life and responsibility, bodily changes, and a keener, more questioning look at things.

"A kid has to weigh everything—school, parents, peers," says Dr. Nicolay, "and make choices as to what is important to him and find ways to live when not all is clear. Too bad there is no magical solution, but if there were, one wouldn't believe it anyway."

What are times you have been under stress?
Have you found a way out of stress—something to do when your world sits on you like a rock?
What kinds of pressures or stresses do your friends have? Is your stress different from theirs?
Are there ways to avoid stress?
Are there times when stress is good?

Stress may not exactly be good, but it is a part of life and its successes. Some jobs, such as that of a reporter, are built on stress. Each day there is a deadline or group of deadlines when news articles have to be written. The deadline assures that something is done.

Among nations, the pressure to surrender can lead to victory or defeat, depending on whose side you are on. It can lead to less bloodshed.

Says Dr. Anita B. Siegman, psychologist and director of counseling services at the University of Southern California, in an article by Judi Marks in *'Teen Magazine* (Feb. 1981): "We can't eliminate stress entirely from our lives, and there are some forms of stress that are desirable." One form of good stress is anticipation. Remember the excitement on Christmas eve—is the gift really going to be under the tree? The pressure is not too different from the pressure to be on stage. The waiting and expecting can bring you joy and hope—attitudes that are good for you.

Stress, like most problems, can be overcome. There are answers and alternatives to stressful situations. What would you advise these eleventh- and twelfth-graders at the Dobbins Vocational Tech School in Philadelphia as they tell of times when they felt they were under stress?

—"I feel that I'm under stress at this moment and have been since school started. I'm usually a B-average student, but this school term mostly all my grades were D's. I feel that this school term is going too quickly and the teachers are pushing the students too hard too fast. It's not that I can't do the work, it's because the teachers don't give you time to understand what has to be done."—Girl, 17.

—"I think I really felt stress this summer when my family and I sat down to talk about college and the grades I should have on my first report card. When the school year finally got under way, I was trying so hard to get all the grades I was supposed to, that some of my grades weren't that good. I think that if my family didn't expect so much of me I would have had higher grades."—Boy, 17.

—"I remember when I was on the pep team and attending classes at the same time. I had the workload of schoolwork, and the responsibility of collecting money for the pep team. I have to be dedicated in everything I do. All the pressure was on me to make sure that the books and the records of the team were up to date."—Girl, 17.

—"When I was in an accident which left a scar on my face, and I was afraid that I will never be myself again, I felt as though no one from the opposite sex will find me attractive. Then it was time for the prom and everyone turned me down. I felt hopeless. I lost my friends, and my interest."—Girl, 17.

—"It was a warm day. Everything started bothering me. Schoolwork, enemies in school, enemies outside, my parents, and staying in my room all the time. I couldn't do anything but cry. I would get several headaches that stayed for about an hour or two each day. I couldn't eat—I stayed sick, awake."—Boy, 17.

—"Once I felt like I was under stress when my pastor died and the choir had to sing Sunday. Visitors had to be fed (from Friday on), the burial was Monday and the refreshments had to be served after the burial, by me and a few others at the church."—Girl, 16.

—"I am under stress right now. My mother has been sick for a long time without anyone knowing it. It has put a lot of pressure on me because I have to take care of her, housework, cook, and also my schoolwork. Even though I try very hard in some classes, I just can't get the hang of things, but with God and everyone else's help I'll get through."—Girl, 17.

—"When my parents were on the verge of splitting up, my grades were going down in school and my boyfriend and I were arguing every day. Just nothing was going my way."—Girl, 17.

—"A typical day could cause stress. But every once in a while one of those days comes where everything goes wrong. You wake up late, there's nothing in the refrigerator to cook quick. You leave to catch the bus. You just miss it. The next one is crowded and it rides past your corner. The next one comes and is equally crowded. You barely get on. The people don't want to move back. Every one bumps you in some way. You finally get to school and you have to wait for the end of the period to go to class. You miss that class. In your next class, you have a surprise test, gym the next period, then lunch. Yipee!"—Boy, 18.

There are many ways to solve some instances of stress, but, of course, when it is just too much, guidance counselors, school psychologists, and other trained adults are there to help.

The teacher of these teens, Esther Jantzen, has this advice for her students when they feel under stress:

1. "Don't procrastinate. Stress is often related to guilt about things left undone."
2. "Schedule some solitude into your week. Being around others all the time is demanding."

Also, when a problem has you clamped down and the pressure is mounting, keep looking for that special solution. Like a good mystery solver, follow the clues and opportunities.

Cindy, in the twelfth grade at the Dobbins Vocational Tech School, did just that. "I had a term paper due in English on March 30," she says, "but I could not type it because my arm got cut on a piece of glass. I was really worried because my teacher kept on saying if I didn't have the report in, I was going to fail the class and this was a college-bound class. So later on I talked to her and she told me I could turn it in no later than April 30, but I was still worried because I didn't have a typewriter at home. The only one I could use was in school and other people have to do their work, too. So my shop teacher let me use the hour and a half we are there for a week so I could type it up. I was so glad because I really liked college English and I hope to do well in it in college. And I got my term paper in on time."

Those who have a "hardiness" or a hard shell to defend against stress are, according to psychologists at the University of Chicago, those who have an openness to change, feel involved in whatever they are doing, and keep a sense of control.

Psychologists used to think that a good bit of illness came from conflicts within—your own thinking, reasoning, and emotional responses. But researchers at the University of Chicago and University of California psychologist Richard

S. Lazarus, in his book *Psychological Stress and the Coping Process* (McGraw-Hill, 1966), see stress as related to outside forces or the environment. If that's the case, some things can be done by controlling or avoiding the outside causes of stress.

Dr. Jackie Schwartz, in her book *Letting Go of Stress* (Pinnacle Books, 1982), suggests breathing in deeply and slowly, to a count of four, and out to a count of eight. She suggests learning to think positively and learning to laugh heartily, thus releasing tension. She also advises controlling anger by identifying it and thinking about it when you are angry.

She suggests, as others do, learning to relax by finding a quiet place without interruption and to enjoy being still for a while.

She also recommends various diet approaches, such as cutting down on sugar and eating more fruit; cutting down on salt and using lemons and herbs.

Dr. Benjamin Feingold, who has written a book on the hyperactive child, believes certain chemicals in food, sometimes causing allergies, can also lead to disturbed mental states and stress in youngsters. His ideas are challenged by some, but most agree that good nutrition feeds both body and mind, and that a healthy body and mind can better handle stress.

Learning that you don't always have to act the same way every time can remove some pressure. A yes answer all the time can mean you're a doormat. Giving in to pressure does not eliminate it, but just makes you a slave to it. On the other hand, rebelling and saying no all the time is not always good either. "The outcome of rebellion is often more pressure," says Judi Marks in *'Teen Magazine* (Feb. 1981). "The rule breaker, for instance, might end up facing more restrictions from the school vice principal, her family, or whatever authority figure she's battling.

"And she won't be developing her own independence in

the meantime. Instead, she's what psychologists call 'counter-dependent.' She'll always be reacting to others' rules (usually in a negative way) instead of learning to set appropriate guidelines for herself.

"Another consequence of rebellion is guilt."

One course of action, Marks suggests, is the "assertive approach." That means asserting yourself and making your true feelings known. If you don't want to go someplace or to loan a book, don't.

"Sometimes teenagers," says Dr. Siegman, "feel.they have to be perfect to be accepted, when in fact no one likes someone who's all that perfect!" Still, as we saw in the chapter on low esteem, it is useful to think of ourselves in terms of being miraculous or perfect in terms of creation.

When Jesus told his hearers to be "perfect" (Matt. 5:48, KJV and many translations), he was using a word that really means "complete" or "completely involved."

Maybe it should be read that way. "Be ye perfect"—that is "Be ye complete, involved." Be involved. Be thoughtful in every situation. Be you. That attitude will get rid of some of the stress.

SWEARING

19

*&¢%$!@!

Three teenagers were standing on a corner.

A car went through the intersection and plowed into another car, and both cars landed piled up on the sidewalk and against a telephone pole. Possibly somebody was hurt. It happened so fast.

The reactions of the three teens were:

The tall one got so excited he shouted a lot of four-letter words. He acted as if he had himself been stunned in the wreck, repeating the words over and over.

The middle-size teen said first of all, "Oh, no," somewhat quietly, and there were hints of some swear words, subdued, as he moved forward to help.

The third teen seemed to be struck dumb by the happening. He just stood there as if frozen and was not heard to swear.

An overreactive person, a rational-thinking person, and one who emotionally is unable to respond: which one would you want standing on the corner when you asked for help?

The first was caught up in his excitement and emotional outburst of words. The second one appeared to be the thinking one. The third was just frozen. A wordless, nonemotional person, he did not really respond.

Language does not tell the whole story about a person, but it does sometimes tell about the type of person one is and the coolheadedness, or lack of it, by which one responds. Language is a mirror of personality.

In older days it was easier to typecast a person by whether or not he or she swore. Swearing was not considered proper. The issue is not so keen as it was, but it is still a subject worth thinking about.

Some people think it is bad to swear all the time.

Some think it is OK to swear on occasion. Others don't worry about it.

Certainly society is much more open about language than it was in 1939 when Clark Gable in *Gone with the Wind* caused a controversy by declaring to Scarlett O'Hara, "Frankly, my dear, I don't give a damn."

Or when editorial writers thirty years ago went after President Harry Truman for using "hell" and "damn" in a speech. One writer then maintained that "only an ignorant man uses profanity" and so profanity was not befitting of the person in the highest office in the land. President Richard Nixon used profanity on his secret tapes. Actually George Washington used some profanity.

Does it make any difference who uses profanity—a junior high student or the President of the United States? A worker in a factory or a pastor of a church?

What's a curse?

Is there anything in common between a mummy's curse calling evil on somebody and a cab driver cursing the driver who cut in front of him?

At the summer day camp in Maple Glen, Pennsylvania, Paul, ten, remarked that when God in the Ten Commandments said, "You shall not make wrong use of the name of the Lord your God'" (Ex. 20:7) God meant all cursing was to be avoided. What do you think?

Is there a difference between "darn" and "damn" and "heck" or "hell"?

Back in 1967, a Baptist minister in Utica, New York, took a job in a factory and he wore a foot-wide sign on his back which said, "The Lord will not leave unpunished the man who misuses his name" (Ex. 20:7). The minister wanted to stop his fellow workers from swearing. Instead, the pastor was fired from the factory job. Do you think he should have been fired?

Some feel that those who swear a lot are telling people they are frustrated or confused, that they are tired of school or a job. Swearing becomes both a release and a way of getting attention.

One psychologist feels a little swearing might have some value, but he also feels that too much of it may be an indication of mental sickness such as schizophrenia. Dr. Chaytor Mason, a professor at the University of Southern California, quoted in *Time* magazine (Dec. 14, 1981), says most kids go through a swearing period using a kind of magic of words to imitate adults and also to test the limits around the home. Mason suggests parents who use occasional swear words talk with kids on why they use them rather than telling kids not to follow their example.

Another doctor who says that excessive and offensive use of bad words might suggest a mental problem or disorder in some is Dr. David V. Forrest, M.D., of the department of psychiatry at Columbia University College of Physicians and Surgeons. He says an alcoholic, or a person on drugs, or a person suffering a stroke might use a horrific vocabulary. Some illnesses bring on a tendency to swear. One neurological condition that appears in childhood or adolescence, he says, is an involuntary tic called Gilles de la Tourette syndrome. "A variety of ticlike movements may be associated, but there also may be nothing but suddenly blurted curse words." Dr. Forrest, quoted in Leonard Gross's *The Parents' Guide to Teenagers*, says "an exaggerated habit of cursing in any young person warrants at least a consultation with a psychiatrist."

The English language, unlike others, has only a few dirty

words and many of these can be heard in the movie theater and at school. Because of the shortage of such words, one writer, Reinhold Aman, suggests in *Time* magazine, Dec. 14, 1981, that one make up his or her own harmless words to let off steam. He points out, according to *Time*, that since most "dirty" words emphasize f, sh, k, p, t, s, and x sounds, you can put together your own harmless combinations with similar sounds, such as "shexing" and " oh fex." To do this, Aman says, will let off steam, confuse many, and offend none. Actually, one popular family TV show did just this. Remember in *Alice*, Flo vented her steam by saying, "Kiss my grits." It sounds awful, but is, apparently, harmless.

"It's kind of neat to be able to use a word that you can't express any other way," says Dr. Barry Ginsberg, school psychologist in Doylestown, Pennsylvania. But, he says, while the word or words you choose might make you feel real good, it might hurt you with other people.

Words have an effect. Words can be insulting or complimentary, mean or happy, out of place or acceptable.

Using swear words in groups may mean that you are telling all that you are a big shot. Or maybe it's just for shock or teasing or to put somebody down. Or maybe it's to say, "I'm with you. You talk that way, so will I."

Do you know anybody who swears in every breath? Is Cynthia Gorney right when she says in *Seventeen* magazine (Jan. 1981), "People who swear all the time are mostly full of fear, uncertainty, or hot air—or sometimes, all three"?

Words have no power, yet we swear our oaths on the Bible for public office, or in court.

Besides the value and honesty of simple language, remember, too, that language is not just yours but is shared.

In John Irving's novel *The Hotel New Hampshire* (Dutton, 1981), a fifteen-year-old, John, is the hero and narrator. He swears awfully; his mother, a suffering silent type, barely tolerates it.

Then the family moves to Europe. The mother and the

younger brother take a different airplane. The mother and the little brother are lost at sea.

John and his surviving sister and older brother, in their grieving, want to do something in memory of the mother. The young hero says:

"I couldn't change enough, and I knew it. All I could do was something that would have pleased Mother. I could give up swearing, I could clean up my language—which upset Mother so. And so I did."

VALUES

20

Topping the List

The auction was about to start.

There were no chairs, tables, TV sets, garden tools, or fine china for sale.

This was an auction of ideas.

"Auctioneer" was Bernie Dunphy-Linnartz, youth leader. The "buyers" were a group of kids in New York State.

They were at a value auction as part of a camp program, and the long list of things before them showed what they valued.

Each buyer had "100 points." The points were to be used like money. Once the 100 points were used up, that was it for each kid.

The top ten things the kids bid their points on were:

—Five close friends for life
—Color TV and stereo in own room
—World peace
—Cleanup of air and water
—Chance to run school for a week
—Good relations with parents
—Spend day with favorite TV character
—Trip around the world
—Ten minutes in a store with a cart or wheelbarrow to take all you can
—$1000

There were other items that were not in the top ten "bought" by the kids, but the big-vote ideas told what the kids thought to be of the most value to them.

Values are like goals. They are something you want, and values, like goals, are things or ideas you want to reach.

Obviously, not everybody has the same values; not all want the same thing. At some points in life, some things are best, but when you are older, you might like something else. Older people might, for instance, put a high value on good health and being young.

Religious groups emphasize different values. One group may put special value on going to heaven; another group might talk about the value of service to others.

What is worth the most to you?
What are the most important values and goals for you?
Can you put your values in order—the most important first, then the second, and so on?
Do some kids have wrong values? How do you know if they do?
How can you find or realize the best values for your life?

Teens at the Dobbins Vocational Tech School in Philadelphia found that they had a lot of values.

Here are their most important values as they answered: "What is worth the most to you?"

—"My art work, because it gives me a sense of pride."—Boy, 17.

—"Having all of my parents alive and in good health."—Girl, 17.

—"Education, because you can't succeed in any job market without a high school education."—Girl, 17.

—"My job because it helps to keep me busy and out of trouble."—Girl, 16.

—"My well-being."—Boy, 17.

—"My family because they are my life."—Girl, 17.

—"Money because you can't live in this world without it."—Girl, 17.

—"Jesus, because without him I would have nothing nor be anything."—Boy, 17.

—"Friends, because friends make life a whole lot easier to go through day after day."—Boy, 16.

—"My personality, because it reflects my true self."—Boy, 18.

—"My pride—without it you cannot stand up to what is right and wrong."—Boy, 19.

—"My body, because it was a special gift that God has given me."—Girl, 17.

—"A friendship with Jehovah God, because by maintaining a good relationship with him, it may gain me everlasting life in a paradise on earth."—Girl, 16.

—"My life and what I do with it, because I believe everyone has something to contribute to the world and they should do their utmost to make the world a little easier to live in."—Girl, 16.

Several others also felt "life" itself was the most important of all, the top value.

—"My life is worth more to me than anything in the world. I feel this way because once you're gone you don't have a good chance of coming back. So I live every day like it was my last."—Girl, 17.

—"My life is worth the most to me. It's the only thing I really can treasure. Material possessions are only things you have. They don't match up to life. Without life you can't have material possessions."—Boy, 17.

"Life" is right up there at the top of kids' minds, youth leaders say. "Kids really do care about being alive," says Ima Jean Kidd, director of Learning Needs, Vacation, Leisure and Outdoor Education for the National Council of Churches. "Life is a high priority in the values of kids, and that includes an appreciation for the potential of life over economic and material values, for instance. Kids are interested in the environment, the global sustaining of life, and the quality of life."

She said that kids, "overawed" with the possibility of nuclear destruction, "realize the sustaining of the universe depends on living together and on justice around the world."

Writers vary as to how seriously they feel kids and teens regard values. One researcher, writing in 1965, found that young people follow their friends in a culture which puts a lot of weight on social and athletic values over others. Comments James F. Adams in *Understanding Adolescence: Current Developments in Adolescent Psychology* (Allyn & Bacon, 1968): "It can be said with some accuracy that adolescents do not have many serious values, or at best that their serious values exert less influence over their everyday behavior than their peer-oriented values."

"It's unfortunate that the traditional model (for values) doesn't hold up in our society," says Dr. Robert M. Krauss. "The traditional type of philosophy of life which tells you what to do gets all clouded up. The sad thing is not only that it (a general philosophy of life) no longer exists, but nothing of substance has replaced it. Materialistic goals become overwhelming."

Yet a poll found that teens, once they've gone through the changing period of adolescence, do settle down with fairly serious values. A Gallup Youth Poll (*The Daily Intelligencer*, May 27, 1982) says that "Jennifer" and "Michael" (most popular names today) are less self-centered than many might think: "Religious belief is one of the most important influences in Michael's and Jennifer's lives, and both teens are members of a church in their hometown. Both teenagers overwhelmingly feel that responsibility, self-respect, and honesty are important qualities for their generation to learn."

The real problem with values—for kids as for adults—is how do you rank values or put one up against the other?

Esther Jantzen is teacher of the eleventh- and twelfth-grade classes at the Dobbins Vocational Tech School in Philadelphia, where the kids named what was most valuable to them. She suggests three things to do in helping to determine values:

1. "Evaluate periodically (say every six months) which things are most important to you. Write them down. Keep a journal.

2. "Try to think in terms of long-range issues.

3. "Read a lot and think about what the author's characters value."

Says Delmar Wedel, the director for international training at the YMCA, New York: "It's important to know who our heroes are, and I would get kids to read."

Sometimes values conflict with each other. How do you know how to choose one value over the other?

If you don't think values are ever in conflict, try these examples from noted Harvard professor Lawrence Kohlberg, as summarized in *Psychology Today* (Feb. 1979):

"There was, for instance, the famous case of Heinz, whose wife is dying and can only be saved by a rare drug; the drug has been discovered by the local pharmacist, who is the sole owner and is charging an exorbitant price that Heinz cannot pay. Should Heinz steal the drug? Does the pharmacist have a right to charge so much for it?

"Another popular Kohlberg story is the dilemma of Sharon, who goes shopping one day with her best friend, Jill. Jill tries on a sweater and walks out of the store wearing it under her coat, leaving Sharon to face a security officer who demands that she tell him the name of the other girl. The owner of the store tells her she will be in serious trouble if she does not report her friend, who, he is sure, has been shoplifting. Should Sharon protect her friend and not reveal her name? Does she really owe anything to Jill, who has walked out and left her in this dilemma?"

Kohlberg believes people go through a half dozen stages of development in learning to cope with the hard decisions. He emphasizes the importance of thinking through a problem and asking such questions as, "What is the best decision in that situation?"

You can think of many situations where there is a conflict of values. It may be wrong to lie, steal, or kill, according to the Ten Commandments and most people's ideas. But if you can save a life by lying, does not the value of life win out over the rule of not lying? An example: An old man has died, but should his wife, who is also sick and might not be able to take the shock of the word of his death, be told? One might tell a white lie instead. In the Heinz story above, maybe it is better to steal. In another scenario, it might be better to shoot a sniper than to let him kill more people. Or to kill a dictator: some people, even religious people, tried to kill German madman Adolf Hitler in the belief that if they succeeded, many lives would be saved and World War II might end earlier.

The choice in deciding what values to follow comes down to:

1. Do what is best in a situation without slavishly conforming to a code. "We all recognize universal principles," says Dr. Krauss, "but it's the implementation that is hard. We drift into certain values, and we all ascribe to 'Do unto others as you would want them to do to you' as Hillel (an ancient rabbi) said (as well as Jesus and other world religious leaders). The trouble is with our analytical ability to provide certain answers, such as, 'But what does it mean in a certain situation?' Think out your actions. Whatever

you do," says Dr. Krauss, "do consciously and not automatically."

2. Rank or put in order your values, so you know which is most important to follow when there is a conflict.

For example, if "life" is the most important, you make your decisions as to what will best preserve life.

Or peace. What will best bring peace. And so on.

Some feel it doesn't make much difference which of the two approaches you follow. In a way they come down to the same thing: do what is best in a situation.

Says psychologist Robert Nicolay: "Values depend on what works in society and what you want. Do you want to be happy and unfamous, or famous and unhappy? Only you know what works.

"You can rank and put values in order, if you wish, if you like to organize things, if you're the kind of guy who likes to organize a toolbox." Then organizing your values may be just for you. If you don't like organizing that much, maybe following one or several basic ideas is enough, such as doing what is the most humanly beneficial and life preserving in each case.

Years ago, writer Edgar Sheffield Brightman was noted for creating ranks of values.

At the very top of his list was a group of values that were wide and included many things, such as our relationships with others. Included were artistic (esthetic) values, religious values, social (friendship, etc.) values, character values (good reputation, etc.), intellectual values (ideas, education).

Then there came values that were lower and more personal, such as work values, recreational values, bodily values.

The lowest group had values that help us to get things done or achieved, "instrumental" values. These include "natural" values such as light, gravity, etc., and work and economic values.

Jesus summed it up for one questioner, a Pharisee, who asked, "Which is the great commandment in the law?"

Jesus said unto him, "Love the Lord your God with all your heart, with all your soul, with all your mind.

"That is the greatest commandment. It comes first.

"The second is like it: Love your neighbor as yourself." (Matt. 22:36–40)

21

Zapping and Jumping for Joy

Have you seen the movie *TRON*?

Jeff Bridges is Flynn, an electronic game player, a designer of computer programs and games. He owns his own arcade. But he ends up in the game, literally, as a tiny participant.

That's because of the development of one Master Control Program (MCP) which knows all the games. Helped by a sinister head of a computer company, the MCP takes over all power and clamps down on Flynn.

"I've gotten 2,415 times smarter," the MCP boasts. Threatened by the genius of Flynn, the MCP announces, "I'll have to put you on the game grid." That is to get rid of the meddling Flynn.

So Jeff Bridges as Flynn is reduced to an electric pulse person inside the complicated games. He not only has to win, like an old-fashioned gladiator, and jump through more worlds than Alice in Wonderland, but like Dorothy in *The Wizard of Oz*, he has to battle witch-like electronic characters until he enters the great godlike smiling funnel and destroys it. When the MCP disintegrates, Bridges materializes back into the real world as a beam works to reassemble his molecules.

With Bridges now smarter than them all, you know he's going to go on and become rich and come up with more games—until somebody steals his secrets again and a central machine gets the upper circuit and seeks to take over the world.

Millions of young people are absorbed with video games. Some 100 million cartridges were expected to be sold to homes in 1982. *Time* magazine (April 26, 1982) predicted that Atari, the biggest supplier of home-video consoles and cartridges, would likely sell $400 million worth of coin-operated video games and some $1.3 billion worth of home video consoles and cartridges. "This represents a revenue for Warner (the parent company of Atari) almost six times that of their record business, five times that of the film division and about 47 times that of their Oscar-winning movie *Chariots of Fire*."

Hundreds of games are on the market, beeping and screeching to life, from home units to the coin-operated monsters in diners, arcades, and campus buildings. Pac-Man, of course, is still right up there. In 1981, *Mad* magazine even named Pac-Man man of the year and put the yellow gobbler on its cover. Now there is Ms. Pac-Man, who also gulps her way to success.

Kids in three states, asked for their most popular games, cited: Donkey Kong, Asteroids, Space Invaders, Stargate, Phoenix, Defender, Kong Gorilla, Night Driver, Space Chase, Combat, Missile Command, Tempest. There are many more, new ones each week: Astrosmash, Adventure, Kaboom, Star Raiders, Protector, Centipede, Battlezone, Lockjaw, Space Cavern, Galaxian, Astro Blaster, Vanguard, Zaxxon, Robotron, Frogger, Pitfall, and so on.

As you know, you can't just sit back and play the games quietly. They're fast, and as you give them your total attention, you can get pretty excited. One kid, from the Cedar Drive School, Colts Neck, New Jersey, says his mother even gets so excited "she throws a tantrum when she loses!"

A Cedar Drive girl, twelve, put it this way: "I was playing Pac-Man in an arcade and I was doing pretty well when I got 'eaten.' Then I started to get pretty poor and mad. When I get mad I get mad. So then I got so good I beat the record and became the champ. A few minutes later the game started to smoke. I was so proud of myself I almost kissed everyone in the place."

Said a boy of thirteen, at the Summit Hill Junior High School in Frankfort, Illinois: "Let me describe my friend Joe. First, he removes the quarter from his hand. He places it into the slot of the Tempest game. He pushes the player button. Then he shoots. He shoots the junk that comes up. When he shoots them all, he goes down the tunnel. He sees the warning sign: 'Watch for Spikes.' The sweat beads on his forehead. He hits the spikes. He yells, curses, because the game is over."

A girl, thirteen, at the Blue Springs (Missouri) Junior High School: "My friend Janet and I used to go play Pac-Man all summer, but we don't as much anymore. When Janet plays, she jumps all over and yells and is just generally embarrassing. So I don't go with her anymore. We spent about six dollars one night. She was playing Pac-Man and she jumped up and when she landed she twisted her ankle and sprained it."

The trouble with the games is that you can get addicted. That is, you're so tied to the games you don't want to do anything else. The kids at Cedar Drive tell of their friends regularly dropping ten dollars at a time and of little brothers and sisters spending all of their allowances as soon as they get them. Some kids become like adult gamblers. They get in deeper and deeper, feeling they have to spend every quarter on the games. Said one twelve-year-old Cedar Drive girl: "Laurie is always playing computer games. She spends so much time there that sometimes she spends over ten dollars a week. I am now getting so discouraged that I hate her when she is playing the games."

Said Carolyn, fourteen, at Blue Springs Junior High: "If you are really addicted to video games, then you usually get all your friends into it, too. It's really hard to quit putting your money in after you have lost for the sixteenth time, and when you're in a losing streak you really do get into a terrible depression. But they really are lots of fun!"

One problem with addiction to the games ιs that you're limiting your life. Says Audrey Brainard, who teaches the sixth grade at the Cedar Drive School: "When addiction occurs, there seems little opportunity for growth: intellectual, interpersonal, emotional, or physical. The importance of expansion and development to the most of one's ability in these areas should be stressed in order to become a fully functioning human being."

She questions whether kids spend too much time playing games designed by others. It's like sports. You ought to participate by creating games of your own, she says, and not spend all the time following other people's patterns.

Delmar Wedel, director of international training for the YMCA, New York, says: "It's a cheap way to get thrills, and I wonder if a young person develops good skills and personality if he or she is addicted to a game."

Actually, kids can develop skills by developing their own games and other fun programs on personal home computers. Summer computer camps for kids are becoming popular. One camp in Solvang, California, teaches kids various computer languages, among them BASIC and FORTRAN, and a kid computer language, LOGO. They learn to use a computer for drawing, even for creating tunes such as the *Star Wars* theme.

One boy who is thinking on his own is George, eleven, from Cedar Drive School: "I do not spend a lot of money. I program my own games. I now am in the middle of copying one of the space games and have made up many of my own games. I know four computer languages. I'm going to try to get a summer job with Bell, working as a computer programmer. I started all this when I used to play Space Invaders all the time."

Says Mike, twelve, of the same school, about his friend: "He really doesn't spend money on Space Invaders, etc. But instead, he bought a home computer (ZX81). He writes his own games for it. Some of the games he makes are better than a game you spend money on. Well, he can sit at the computer for a while and then he starts to type and he has a game."

Of course you can be addicted to the home computer just as to a coin-operated one. Says one girl, also a member of the Cedar Drive sixth-grade class: "My friend spends a lot of time at the computer and making games. He is like a baby with a stuffed animal."

Time magazine (May 3, 1982) tells the story of one computer "nerd" or truly addicted fan from Lexington, Massachusetts. The sixteen-year-old got so deeply absorbed by the terminal after school, his parents had a hard time getting him to meals. His father solved the problem by going to the cellar and pulling the main power switch for the house, cutting off the computer's power.

The question of violence comes up when people talk about the video games. Does all that zapping of creatures and aliens encourage kids and adults to be more violent?

Dr. Herbert R. Adams, an educator in Chicago, says: "We do what the payoff is. If the payoff is for destroying, we then want to become better at destroying. Wow! I can destroy 13 million space invaders. Somebody else can destroy only 12 million. So you go out able to destroy." Dr. Adams wonders whether the dedication to destroying on a grand scale carries over to the rest of life.

In all the zapping and killing on the video game screen, there is another interesting point to consider. All the "killing" is very general or anonymous. You're not killing anybody personally. On the one hand, this might suggest that the computer game addict does not transfer hostility at the screen to real people individually. On the other hand, killing anonymously, without feeling one is killing a person, is at the root of some horrors of our modern age. The staffs of the death camps of Adolf Hitler regarded people as groups and destroyed them as casually as if they were insects; and in Vietnam, death rained from the air on villages and groups of people. And it was the same in the big bombing raids of World War II: bombardiers did not see the enemy as individuals. Such an approach made it easier to kill.

Zapping in the old days was done by kids playing Cowboys and Indians, bang-banging one another. "One would 'shoot' and the other would fall out of the saddle," Dr. Robert M. Krauss of Columbia University recalls. "In some ways video games are like that."

But to Dr. Krauss the games, when you come right down to it, are not really frightening. The games in their settings remind him of the pool halls of your parents and grandparents. "These video games are more akin to pool— games of skill," he says. "And there is an obvious positive side—computers become a part of the kid's life," preparing him for the future.

Parents in the old days did not like pool and kept kids from pool halls, just as many parents keep kids from arcades today. "Interestingly, each generation finds something wrong with the pursuits young people enjoy the most," Dr. Krauss says. "Pool was sinful, so was pinball. But there are worse things. Kids could be doing other things."

To give yourself wholeheartedly to something, even games, builds you to a high level of enthusiasm, makes you think as you seek to win. "It is charming, yes, and creative, to be totally absorbed," says Dr. Krauss. He points out that a person absorbed with the games might later bring the same concentration to his or her career and become a big success.

Says *Time* magazine: "The precise orderly steps of logic required to use and program the machines promise to shape and sharpen the thought processes of the computer generation. Indeed, the youngsters playing all those strategy games are doing precisely what corporations do when they plan to launch a new product or what military leaders do when they devise strategies to confront a potential foe."

But sharpening logical abilities and the mind is not all that life is about. The *Time* cover story on computers and kids asks if clear thinking is enough—if, in fact, there might not be a danger in raising a generation to believe that it has the tools to analyze any problem. Says Joseph Weizenbaum, a computer science professor at the Massachusetts Institute of Technology: "There's a whole world of real problems, of human problems, which is essentially being ignored." We can't very well reduce a human relationship to a print-out or solve a moral question by bits and bytes.

The same point is made by Rabbi Steven M. Fink, Elkins Park, Pennsylvania: "There are children who spend hours with these things, who forget the sound of a human voice, the feeling of a warm touch, the joy of friendship, and also the stresses and strains of human interaction. They wrap themselves up in a cocoon and cut off contact with the outside world." (*Philadelphia Inquirer*, Oct. 20, 1982)

If you're going to play the games, kids in the three schools in Illinois, Missouri, and New Jersey suggest:

1. "Have a schedule, like play on Monday, Wednesday, and Friday."

2. "Make a limit how much you can spend."

3. "Play one game less every time you go to the arcade, until you are down to one game, and spend your money elsewhere."

4. "Spend some time doing other things. Find other hobbies and friends that like other things besides just computer games."

5. "Learn computer programming and develop your own games."

WINNING/LOSING

22

Going for the Gusto

Suppose there were no "first" or "best" in life, no winners and no way to tell if something was best.

Everything from national government to sports and entertainment would be different. Lincoln might have been only some obscure lawyer. In fact, the idea of a president would be out of order, for the office is the "first" in our land. There would be no superbowls in sports, no cheering, and there would be a kind of "Who cares?" attitude. People would be more like vegetables than people.

If there weren't men and women who wanted to be the first ones over the mountains and across the seas, if there weren't people who wanted to invent something previously unknown, who wanted to excel in leadership and write and draw new and more interesting things, we would still be living in caves.

But strangely, not enough kids want to be first or best anymore, says Dan McKee, assistant pastor at the large Fourth Presbyterian Church in Chicago.

"Kids don't have heroes they want to be like," he says. "There is an air of anti-heroes. I do not see overachievers, but rather, a 'so what?' attitude. The bad guy wins and often nobody cares."

Striving to be first, striving to be best, even at great cost, is a part of what life is about.

There are little firsts in our daily rituals, such as brushing our teeth first thing in the morning. And other firsts: the first flower in the garden, the first airplane ride, the first day in a new school or new room or with a new teacher. There are bigger and rarer firsts—such as an achievement, becoming an officer of a club, or a first job. We all need to be first in something, if only to be the first one in a household or on a job to smile in the morning.

There are a lot of firsts to strive for at school and in other activities. Kids in two schools—one in a small town, Barryton, Michigan, one in Philadelphia, Pennsylvania—each had firsts to strive for.

The firsts toward which they strove ranged all the way from being first in sports or band to an essay writing contest. One thirtèen-year-old in Barryton said she tried to be first "in getting guys, 'cause if you're first, you have a better chance in getting along with them."

As weird as that last remark might be, it shows that reaching goals is important. But being first need not mean you are in competition. A first for you, an attainment, is what is important.

Said a farm boy from the Chippewa Hills Junior High School in Barryton: "I wanted to be first in something, and I was first. It was a wrestling match, and I wanted to win bad. If someone doesn't want to be first in their life, they've got a problem."

Is that true, that one has a problem if he or she doesn't want to be first?

Is there some time when you want to be last?

What did Jesus mean when he said, "If anyone wants to be first, he must make himself last of all and servant of all" (Mark 9: 35)?

But even though he said that, he also said, "Be ye therefore perfect" (Matt. 5: 48, KJV), and that sounds like asking you to do your best. How do you reconcile the two statements: to be "last" and to be "perfect"?

What is your "best"?

What is your "worst"? Is there any way of changing it into some kind of "best" for you?

Just as not trying to be first might be a problem, trying too hard might be a problem as well. You don't want to try so hard you forget everything else—even your friends.

When you strive to be first, the city kids and rural kids say:

1. "Do not be first at any price."
2. "Respect others for wanting the same thing."
3. "Do not want it so much you feel destroyed if you don't get it."
4. "Make sure you play it straight. Don't break any rules or cheat."
5. "Think of others before yourself."
6. "Just because you may be better, don't put others down. Never think of yourself as the king and others as serfs."
7. "Keep trying. Don't give up. Practice makes perfect."
8. "Give it all you got."
9. "Be fair."
10. "Don't build all of your life on being first, because no one is first all the time."
11. "Have a lot of self-confidence."
12. "Take chances."
13. "Never give up."
14. "Think positive."
15. "Meet the right people, so you have help if needed."
16. "Have a pleasant disposition."
17. "Learn to accept defeat."
18. "Be original. Use your creativity."
19. "Go after something you're good in."
20. "Finish what you start."

With these pointers in mind, remember that *losers are not failures*. For instance, consider the examples of these students at William Penn High School in Philadelphia:

—"Last year I wanted to be the first in high school to win the city division championship in gymnastics on the balance beam. As it turned out, several other girls had beaten my score by 2.4 points. I felt very hurt at first, but I knew I did my best in the event."—Girl, 15, a member of the swimming team, too.

—"I always have and will want to be first. I was raised in an environment where being second isn't good enough; go for the gusto or don't go at all. There are times when I've been second or worse, and, if I give 110 percent of myself, then lose, I'm not a failure. But if I don't go all out, I've already lost."—Boy, 17, who wants to be an actor, comedian, or dancer, and appears regularly on two Philadelphia area dance shows.

—"I've wanted to be first in my dance class because I really love to dance. I tried very hard to overpower my abilities and overworked myself. I wasn't first in the eyes of the dance instructor, but from my standpoint, I was first. Because I kept trying."—Girl, 14, a clarinet player.

—"I always want to be first. One time I was running for the 'youth of the year' at my church. I tried to help everybody I could, just for the award. But the real award came from making people happy. Now I'm not too concerned about who's first, because when I make someone smile, I am always first."—Boy, 16, who likes to sing.

23

Wings in the Wind

The young scholar decided to go around the world to find happiness. He started talking to people, but he didn't find any really happy people, so he decided to talk with the animals. Maybe there was a happy creature someplace.

"Mr. Pig," he said at the first barn, "are you happy?"

"Oink don't know," said the pig, pulling his snout up from the slop. "I have all I want to eat, but I really don't have much fun."

And so the young man went along.

"Mr. Horse, how happy are you?"

The horse was panting, but he said, "I can run real fast . . . wait a minute and watch, but I wish I could sleep in a bed at night."

Then the groundhog looked up from his burrow. "There are a lot of mysterious things in the ground, and I don't have to work much. I just lie around."

"Are you happy?"

"Well, I wish I could jump or fly or make a lot of noise."

And so the young man kept looking. The owl could see at night, the kangaroo had some great dance steps, the mink had a beautiful coat, but they wanted other things. A dog got too hot when he played; a lion had a mean temper and few friends; a monkey acted and looked like a monkey; a penguin's idea of fun was a refrigerator packed with ice; an earthworm had to worry about kids going fishing and the robins. . . .

The young man said, "Maybe I should talk to the birds."

The crow had such an ugly voice, he couldn't be very happy, and the blue jays were pretty, but what a nasty temper. Robins, maybe. "Mr. Robin, are you happy?"

The bird cocked his eye toward the ground. "Would you really be happy watching the ground all day and pulling up and *eating* these stubborn worms?"

Then the swifter and faster birds flew by. The hawk swooped down and devoured a little mouse. "Sometimes it makes me want to cry," said the hawk. He wasn't happy.

Then there were the doves—they were too timid; the pigeons, too nervous.

The swallow seemed happy enough, but spent too much time escaping the high-flying ospreys and hawks.

"Ah, Mr. Wild Canary," said the young man.

The canary, a gorgeous yellow with a touch of black, had beauty; he had song and he sang his heart out; he had food, grain, and berries everywhere, and oh, could he fly—triple somersaults, flittering, and diving. It was hard to get him to sit still long enough to talk to.

"Mr. Canary—you're such a beautiful bird, so musical, so gifted on wings, the world is yours. You seem so happy. Are you happy?"

The little bird twitted and seemed to smile, music welling up in its lungs. He seemed about ready to fly. Indeed, he was already flying when he said it: "Who needs happi ness?" And he was gone on his merry way.

"Happiness takes care of itself," says a quiet, happy, elderly man who likes to relax in Temple University's faculty club in Philadelphia. Dr. Hubert Hamilton, retired chairman of the psychology department at Temple University, at seventy-nine thinks you can talk too much about happiness. "I don't see how you can describe happiness," he said. "Just growing up is happiness. If you're living and doing and enjoying life, you're happy."

Happiness indeed is a hard thing to put into words. You can play little games such as "Happiness is . . ." and come up with all kinds of answers, some of them very funny.

But happiness is as fleeting as the happy little canary, who doesn't know what you are talking about when you talk about happiness.

And happiness is difficult to experience all the time, even if you know when you have it.

"The most we can hope for are moments of happiness," says Irma L. Stahl, teen program consultant for the National Board of the YWCA. Certainly it is hard to find a happy moment during moments of sickness, death, or disappointments.

So who's happy? Who has the happy moments?

Who's happy even though they might not know it?

Kids at schools in Connecticut and Pennsylvania were asked about happy people they might know.

The eighth- and ninth-graders at the Long Lots Junior High School in Westport, Connecticut, each told about the happiest person they know:

—"A senior. He has to work to pay for his college education, and he also has to work hard at school. He's always working and never has time for anything else. If he's lucky, he gets four hours of sleep at night, but everytime I see him he's happy and energetic. I'll never know why."—Girl, 15.

—"The priest at my church. He cares about people and is always smiling. One time a group of kids went to a Grateful Dead concert and got him a shirt. He wears it all the time to show how much he cares."—Girl, 14.

—"Jennifer. She has this boy she's been in love with for a long time. He is a very good guy to have and I wouldn't mind having him myself."—Girl, 15.

—"My father. He is not happy because of something that happened in his life, but just because he has a good life."—Girl, 15.

—"My parents. They don't get in fights or argue. They are having a good time."—Boy, 15.

—"My sister. She laughs about everything."—Boy, 15.

—"A little baby in her playpen."—Girl, 13.

—"Kermit the Frog."—Girl, 13.

—"My science teacher. He always comes into homeroom with a huge smile and leaves school with a huge smile—he's a very fun person to be with."—Boy, 14.

—"Martina. She is always telling jokes and makes everyone laugh."—Girl, 14.

Students in the seventh grade at the Eisenhower Middle School in Norristown, Pennsylvania, had some of the same kinds of happy friends and relatives. In addition, one mentioned an aunt who won $8,000; another, a friend who enjoys dancing; a cousin, one of seven children who gets everything she wants; a nephew allowed into the Cub Scouts although he hasn't reached the required age.

Both schools had students who mentioned "Me" as the happiest.

At the Long Lots School, in Westport, Connecticut:

—"Me. You see, in my school happiness is hard to find, anywhere. I make my own happiness. I joke around and that makes me happy. Being in plays and singing and dancing make me happy."—Boy, 14.

—"Me. Friday night I was happier than I have been in a long time. Because I discovered what God is doing in my life right now. He's preparing me for some trials. I am happy because I have a friend named Jesus. He loves me so much that he died on the cross for me. He is always there when I need him.'—Girl, 15.

At the Norristown, Pennsylvania, school, the happiest person in many cases was also "Me":

—"I'm so happy, because I get everything I want."—Boy, 13.

—"The happiest person in the world is me, because I went over to my cousin's house and he showed me how to mix. We went over to this party and he let me mix (engineer the music equipment) and I turned that party out."—Boy, 14.

—"I was the happiest person I know because when my mom said that she was buying me more designer jeans, I went crazy. I started to kiss her and hug her!"—Girl, 12.

—"I'm the happiest person I know—I'm living, I'm healthy. I have all my family people I love, and I have everything I need and can get everything I want."—Boy, 13.

—"I won third place in a national Show Biz contest. That means I'm third best in the nation."—Boy, 13.

—"I'm the happiest person I know, because last week I got a trophy for track. I ran against nine people in Philly and won the first place trophy."—Girl, 13.

—"The happiest person I know is me, because I made two school teams as a seventh-grader."—Boy, 12.

Who do you think really is the happiest among the kids above?
Are you happy?
Does what makes you happy differ from what makes your friends happy?
What is the best kind of happiness, the kind that lasts the longest?
Could you be happier?

Students at the two schools, in Westport, Connecticut, and in Norristown, Pennsylvania, guessed at what they would like to see happen to make them the happiest persons in the world:

From Norristown's Eisenhower Middle School:

—"To go to a big party and D.J. with my friend, so we could make everybody's feet move to the disco beat."—Boy, 13.

—"To have all the clothes in the world and to be a model."—Girl, 12.

—"To be a full-time singer. I'm only a weekend singer now."—Boy, 13.

—"If I could win some money, like $10 million."—Girl, 13.

—"To make a professional team."—Boy, 12.

—"If I was selected to mix at Circus City (teen disco club in Philadelphia), I would be very happy, because I'd turn it out and the party would be rock'n."—Boy, 12.

—"To get everything you want."—Girl, 12.

—"If my grandmother was alive to see me and to see my youngest brother, because she passed away before he was born."—Girl, 12.

—"For the girl who is mad at me to forgive me. . . . The boy I like to ask me out. . . . My grandfather to live for a while longer."—Girl, 12.

—"A trip to Florida with my family."—Girl, 12.

—"If I had a whole bunch of friends and if when I grow up, I become a nurse. That has been a lifelong dream for me."—Girl, 12.

From the Westport school:

—"Give me a computer, my own house, a motorcycle, and three-week trip to the Virgin Islands."—Boy, 14.

—"Having a girlfriend who cared about me. Someone who doesn't need drugs, smoking, or drinking to make them happy. Or having my own film produced. Of course,

I would have written, starred, and directed it myself."—
Boy, 14.

—"If no one smokes in the world."—Girl, 13.

—"If I could get first honors."—Girl, 13.

—"Straight A's, my family be kept from trouble, and we were granted immortality."—Boy, 13.

—"A dirt bike!"—Boy, 14.

—"Get my band signed by a record company."—Boy, 13.

—"If people would respect me the way I try to respect them and world peace."—Boy, 13.

—"To see Jesus face to face before I see him when I die."—Girl, 15.

—"Having a boyfriend that I'm madly romantically in love with would help, and he'd feel the same about me."—
Girl, 15.

—"To go pro in soccer."—Boy, 15.

—"To score with a girl for the first time."—Boy, 15.

—"If we lived as long as I wanted."—Girl, 15.

—"Get out of adolescence—and get a boyfriend!"—Girl, 14.

The Kennedy family always exhibits a certain amount of exuberance, charisma, and zest for life, and, despite more than a measure of tragedy as well as more than a measure of success, seems to enjoy life—sports, family, and politics. Senator Edward Kennedy was at the head table of the World Future Society meeting in Washington, preparing to give a speech. "How can one be happy in the future?" he was asked. The answer he preferred, he said, would "probably be (one) that the Greeks used. The key (to happiness) would be the exercise of one's talents for others." In other words, he said, happiness would be "along the lines of happiness for others."

Kennedy's idea of acting for others is hard to fault. Even a corporation officer must relate to the personal needs of others if he is to find any happiness. James L. Kraft, founder of the Kraft Foods Company, sought to give away all he could. He gave totem poles to the city of Chicago for parks, helped to purchase and build up the American Baptist conference center at Green Lake, Wisconsin, bought a mountain of jade to cut up in his basement workshop to give away in rings and jewelry, and supported service projects of his own overseas. And he befriended people he found on the street. He had his share of unhappiness in his life, including death by cancer, but his measure of happiness was his capacity to care for others.

James Cone, professor at Union Theological Seminary, New York, says: "Happiness is: You're committed to something that extends beyond yourself. As Martin Luther King used to say, you have to find something worth dying for.

"You're not happy unless you make the commitment that others have the same privileges you have. It's so easy to keep the baby instinct of selfishness. Unfortunately, we live in a society that supports selfishness."

Dr. Cone believes you can find happiness by finding ways to help your friends and by linking up with groups that work for justice and peace. Dr. Cone sees churches or synagogues as places to begin to seek happiness, as members work with the poor and for causes to better the world."

The world is like a family. A family and its members are very unhappy when each one is selfish, so is humanity, Dr. Cone believes. "We are made to live in community," not each one for himself or herself.

Says Dan McKee, youth leader at the Fourth Presbyterian Church in Chicago: "Happiness is self-forgetting. We take ourselves too seriously. We are such burdens to ourselves."

Says Irma Stahl, teen program consultant, National Board of the YWCA: "Happiness can be achieved through connecting with other people—in whatever form we choose—and having control of our lives and using it to create a more just world."

Says Ima Jean Kidd, director of Learning Needs, Vacation, Leisure and Outdoor Education for the National Council of Churches:

"Happiness is liking yourself, liking to be alone with yourself and also in doing things for other people. For some, fulfillment is a better word, the joy of overcoming some difficulty, seeing work completed." Happiness also includes a dimension of surprise, she said. "Something happening that you didn't expect, having fun."

Said author Faith Baldwin, when asked about happiness: "The three things that make me happiest are friends, family, and work. But friends have to include wild birds."

Acknowledgments

Many persons provided useful ideas and contacts in the preparation of this book and to them and those who played special roles, thanks are due.

In addition to several dozen guidance counselors and principals who suggested topics for the book, two groups of people played an important role: the experts in family and the adolescent and pre-adolescent life, and schoolteachers across the country who probed for the problems and self-help suggestions from kids themselves.

Among the experts who kindly consented to interviews:

Herbert R. Adams, director, Secondary School Division, Science Research Associates, Chicago, Ill.

Charles L. Bassman, clinical psychologist, Marlton, N.J.

Tom B. Bate, child abuse caseworker, public defender office, State of New Jersey, Camden, N.J.

Milton E. Block, child psychiatrist, Haddonfield, N.J.

James H. Cone, professor of systematic theology, Union Theological Seminary, New York, N.Y.

Debbie Denny, ethnographer, researcher in "Early Adolescent Study," Institute for Juvenile Research, Department of Mental Health, State of Illinois, Chicago, Ill.

Salvatore Didato, psychologist, New York, N.Y.

Bernie Dunphy-Linnartz, co-director, Youth Program, United Presbyterian Church, New York, N.Y.

Barry Ginsberg, school psychologist, Doylestown, Pa.

Doris E. Hadary, project director, Lab Science and Art for Handicapped Children, professor of chemistry, American University, Washington, D.C.

Hubert Hamilton, retired, psychology department chairman, Temple University, Philadelphia, Pa.

Larry E. Kalp, secretary for Older Childhood Education, Board for Homeland Ministries, United Church of Christ, New York, N.Y.

Ima Jean Kidd, director, Learning Needs, Vacation, Leisure and Outdoor Education, National Council of Churches, New York, N.Y.

Robert M. Krauss, chairman, psychology department, Columbia University, New York, N.Y.

Phyllis Marcuccio, editor, *Science and Children*, Washington, D.C.

Dan McKee, assistant pastor for Christian education, Fourth Presbyterian Church, Chicago, Ill.

Tony Meade, researcher, Institute for Juvenile Research, Department of Mental Health, State of Illinois, Chicago, Ill.

Richard Myers, manager, editorial development, Science Research Associates, Chicago, Ill.

Robert Nicolay, professor of psychology, Loyola University, Chicago, Ill.

Joseph R. Novello, director, Child and Adolescent Services, The Psychiatric Institute, Washington, D.C.

Irma Stahl, teen program consultant, National Board of the YWCA, New York, N.Y.

Delmar Wedel, director, International and Coordinating Services, New York Management Resource Center, YMCA of Greater New York, New York, N.Y.

Randy Wessel, police liaison, "Junior High Study," Institute for Juvenile Research, Department of Mental Health, State of Illinois, Chicago, Ill

The teachers who helped to survey some twelve hundred students in their schools include:

Suzan Young Bramley, Buckingham Elementary, Buckingham, Pa.

Audrey H. Brainard, Cedar Drive School, Colts Neck, N.J.

Margrette R. Davis, FAMU High, Tallahassee, Fla.

Alice H. Cortner, Gina Rives, Vicki Wyatt, Noel Leeney, Cathy Hunt, Clarksville Academy, Clarksville, Tenn.

Martin Tafel, Long Lots Junior High, Westport, Conn.

David Middleton, Summit Hill Senior High, Frankfort, Ill.

Carol Quackenbush, Blue Springs Junior High, Blue Springs, Mo.

Bettie Smith, Apalachee Elementary, Tallahassee, Fla.

Don Hicks, Bob Rubino, John T. Roberts Elementary, Syracuse, N.Y.

Jeanne Goemer, Hosterman Junior High, New Hope, Minn.

Nancy Yarrick, Chippewa Hills Junior High, Barryton, Mich.

Mel Susman, William Penn High, Philadelphia, Pa.

Kristina Kennedy, Westtown Friends School, Westtown, Pa.

Richard Cole, Benton Consolidated High, Benton, Ill.

John D. Wahman, North Junior High, St. Cloud, Minn.

Esther Jantzen, Dobbins Vocational Technical High, Philadelphia, Pa.

Linda Ennis, Thomas Richards School, Atco, N.J.

Bonita Kent Hadrick, Maryann DiDomenici, Marilyn Casey, Patrick Mancini, Eisenhower Middle School, Norristown, Pa.

Bibliography

Here are books for kids—and families—that will be helpful in understanding and facing problems.

Abata, Russell M. *How to Develop a Better Self-Image.* Ligouri Publications, 1980.

Adair, James R., ed. *Unhooked: Dramatic Stories of Persons Who Became Addicted to Drugs but Came Back.* Baker Book House, 1971.

Adams, James F. *Understanding Adolescence: Current Developments in Adolescent Psychology.* 2d ed. Allyn & Bacon, 1973.

Asquith, Stewart. *Children and Justice: Decision-Making in Children's Hearings and Juvenile Courts.* Columbia University Press, 1982.

Beck, Hubert F. *The Cults: How to Respond. . . .* Concordia, 1977.

Belle, Deborah, ed. *Lives in Stress.* Sage Publications, 1982.

Berger, Melvin. *Computers in Your Life.* Thomas Y. Crowell, 1981.

Berne, Eric. *Games People Play.* Ballantine Books, 1964.

Booher, Dianna Daniels. *Coping: When Your Family Falls Apart.* Julian Messner, 1979.

Bradley, Buff. *Endings: A Book About Death.* Addison-Wesley, 1979.

———. *Where Do I Belong? A Kids' Guide to Stepfamilies.* Addison-Wesley, 1982.

Bramnick, Lea, and Simon, Anita. *The Parent's Solution Book*. Franklin Watts, 1982.

Briscoe, Jill. *How to Fail Successfully*. Fleming H. Revell, 1982.

Bromley, David G., and Shupe, Anson D. *Strange Gods: The Great American Cult Scare*. Beacon Press, 1982.

Buchanan, Neal, and Chamberlain, Eugene. *Helping Children of Divorce*. Broadman Press, 1982.

Chapman, A. H. *Parents Talking, Kids Talking*. G. P. Putnam's Sons, 1979.

Claesson, Bent H. *Boy Girl–Man Woman: An Intelligent Guide to Sex Education for Young People*. M. Boyars, 1981.

Clarke, Jean. *Self-Esteem: A Family Affair*. Winston Press, 1978.

Collins, Gary R. *Give Me a Break: The How-to-Handle Pressure Book for Teenagers*. Fleming H. Revell, 1982.

Dauw, Dean C. *Increasing Your Self Esteem: How to Feel Better About Yourself*. Waveland Press, 1980.

Didato, Salvatore. *Psychotechniques*. Methuen, 1980.

Elkins, Dov P. *Twelve Pathways to Feeling Better About Yourself*. Growth Association, 1980.

Enroth, Ronald. *The Lure of the Cults*. Christian Herald Books, 1979.

Fast, Julius. *Body Language*. Pocket Books, 1981.

Finsand, Mary Jane. *Caring and Cooking for the Hyperactive Child*. Sterling, 1981.

Gardner, Richard A. *The Boys and Girls Book About Stepfamilies*. Bantam Books, 1982.

Gilbert, Sara. *How to Live with a Single Parent*. Lothrop, Lee & Shepard, 1982.

Ginott, Haim G. *Between Parent and Teenager*. Avon, 1973.

Gottesman, David M. *The Powerful Parent: A Child Advocacy Handbook*. Prentice-Hall, 1982.

Green, Janet. *Us: Inside a Teenage Gang*. Hastings House, 1982.

Greening, Tom, and Hobson, Dick. *Instant Relief: The Encyclopedia of Psychological Self-Help.* Seaview Books, 1979.

Greenwald, Jerry. *Be the Person You Were Meant to Be.* Dell, 1971.

Grimes, Howard. *How to Become Your Own Best Self.* Word Books, 1979.

Gross, Leonard H., ed. *The Parents' Guide to Teenagers.* Macmillan, 1981.

Hart, Archibald D. *Children and Divorce: What to Expect—How to Help.* Word Books, 1982.

Hauck, Paul A. *Overcoming Jealousy and Possessiveness.* Westminster Press, 1981.

Haven, Barbara Shook. *Very Shy.* Human Sciences Press, 1982.

Henderson, Martha Gray. *Being a Kid Ain't Easy.* Abingdon Press, 1977.

Howard, Marion. *Did I Have a Good Time? Teenage Drinking.* Continuum, 1982.

Hyde, Margaret O. *Addictions.* McGraw-Hill, 1982.

———. *Computers Who Think: The Search for Artificial Intelligence.* Enslow, 1978.

———. *Cry Softly! The Story of Child Abuse.* Westminster Press, 1980.

———. *Mind Drugs.* McGraw-Hill, 1981.

Jensen, Eric. *Student Success Secrets.* Barron's, 1982.

Kelly, Robert. *How Do I Make Up My Mind, Lord: Story Devotions for Boys.* Augsburg, 1981.

Kennedy, Eugene. *On Being a Friend.* Continuum, 1982.

Kiley, Dan. *Keeping Kids Out of Trouble.* Warner Books, 1979.

Koile, Earl. *Your Secret Self.* Word Books, 1978.

Kuczen, Barbara. *Childhood Stress: Don't Let Your Child Be a Victim.* Delacorte Press, 1982.

Laklan, Carol. *Golden Women: Career Women Who Did What They Wanted To.* McGraw-Hill, 1982.

Lauton, Barry, and Freese, Arthur S. *The Healthy Adolescent: A Parents' Manual.* Charles Scribner's Sons, 1981.

Lavender, John Allan. *Beat the Blues: God's Cure for Depression.* Tyndale, 1982.

LeShan, Eda J. *Learning to Say Good-by: When a Parent Dies.* Avon, 1976.

MacKenzie, John. *Be Good to Yourself.* Ross Books, 1980.

Madison, Arnold. *Smoking and You.* Julian Messner, 1975.

McCoy, Kathleen. *Coping with Teenage Depression: A Parent's Guide.* New American Library, 1982.

McCoy, Kathy, and Wibbelsman, Charles, M.D. *The Teenage Body Book.* Pocket Books, 1978.

Mark, Jan. *Nothing to Be Afraid Of.* Harper & Row, 1982.

Mayle, Peter. *Divorce Can Happen to the Nicest People.* Macmillan, 1980.

Miller, Mary Susan. *Childstress! Understanding and Answering Stress Signals of Infants, Children and Teenagers.* Doubleday, 1982.

Moorman, Lawrence, and Jones, Marilyn P. *Becoming Whole: A Self-Help Guide.* 2d ed. Kendall-Hunt, 1979.

Myers, Irma, and Myers, Arthur. *Why You Feel Down—and What You Can Do About It.* Charles Scribner's Sons, 1982.

Narramore, Bruce. *Adolescence Is Not an Illness: A Book for Parents.* Fleming H. Revell, 1980.

Narramore, Clyde M. *Improving Your Self Confidence.* Zondervan, n.d.

Norman, Jane, and Harris, Myron. *The Private Life of the American Teenager: Over 160,000 Teenagers Reveal What They Think—and Really Do: The Norman-Harris Report.* Rawson Wade, 1981.

Oraker, James R., and Meredith, Char. *Almost Grown: A Christian Guide for Parents of Teenagers.* Harper & Row, 1980.

Osgood, Don. *Pressure Points: How to Deal with Stress.* Christian Herald Books, 1980.

Petersen, William J. *Those Curious Cults in the 80s.* Keats, 1982.

Phillips, Beeman N. *School Stress and Anxiety.* Human Sciences Press, 1978.

Podolsky, Edward. *The Jealous Child.* Philosophical Library, 1954.

Rice, F. Philip. *Morality and Youth: A Guide for Christian Parents.* Westminster Press, 1980.

Ridenour, Fritz. *What Teenagers Wish Their Parents Knew About Kids.* Word Books, 1982.

Rinzler, Carol Eisen. *Your Adolescent: An Owner's Manual.* Atheneum, 1981.

Roberts, William O. *Initiation to Adulthood: An Ancient Rite of Passage in Contemporary Form.* Pilgrim Press, 1982.

Rofes, Eric. *The Kids' Book of Divorce: By, For and About Kids.* Vintage, 1982.

Rowlands, Peter. *Saturday Parent: A Book for Separated Families.* Continuum, 1982.

Schaefer, Charles E., and Millman, Howard L. *How to Help Children with Common Problems.* Van Nostrand Reinhold, 1980.

Schafer, Walt. *Stress, Distress and Growth.* International Dialogue Press, 1978.

Seltzer, Vivian Center. *Adolescent Social Development: Dynamic Functional Interaction.* D. C. Heath, 1982.

Shanks, Anne Zane. *Busted Lives: Dialogues with Kids in Jail.* Delacorte Press, 1982.

Shedd, Charlie W., ed. *You Are Somebody Special.* McGraw-Hill, 1978.

Simon, John B. *To Become Somebody: Growing Up Against the Grain of Society.* Houghton Mifflin, 1982.

Simon, Nissa. *Don't Worry, You're Normal.* Crowell Junior Books, 1982.

Smith, Lendon. *Food for Healthy Kids.* Berkley Books, 1981.

Stocking, S. Holly; Arezzo, Diana; and Leavitt, Shelley. *Helping Kids Make Friends.* Argus, 1980.

Strommen, Merton. *Five Cries of Youth*. Harper & Row. 1974.

Twerski, Abraham. *Like Yourself: And Others Will Too.* Prentice-Hall, 1978.

Vickery, Donald M., M.D. *Life Plan for Your Health*. Addison-Wesley, 1978.

Vogel, Jerome. *A Stress Test for Children*. Keats, 1982.

Vogel, Linda Jane. *Helping a Child Understand Death*. Fortress Press, 1978.

Walters, Richard P. *Anger: Yours, Mine and What to Do About It*. Zondervan, 1981.

Weisinger, Hendrie, and Lobsenz, Norman M. *Nobody's Perfect: How to Give Criticism and Get Results*. Stratford Press, 1981.

Welles, Leigh. *Leigh Welles' Ballet Body Book*. Bobbs-Merrill, 1982.

Welter, Paul. *How to Help a Friend*. Tyndale, 1978.

Wright, Norman. *Improving Your Self-Image*. Harvest House, 1977.

Yarbrough, Tom. *How to Be Happy with Yourself: A Guide to Overcome Depression and Failure*. Libra, 1975.

Zeller, William. *Understanding and Accepting Ourselves and Others*. Franciscan Herald Press, n.d.

Zelnik, Melvin; Kantner, John F.; and Ford, Kathleen. *Sex and Pregnancy in Adolescence*. Sage Publications, 1981.

Zerafa, Judy. *Go For It: How to Take Charge of Your Own Life*. Workman, 1982.

Zimbardo, Philip G. *Shyness: What It Is—What to Do About It*. Addison-Wesley, 1977.

Zimring, Franklin E. *The Changing Legal World of Adolescence*. Free Press, 1982.

Index

About the Author

HILEY H. WARD is the author of ten nonfiction books for adults and children and has edited several national magazines for young people. His travels as a writer and reporter have taken him to assignments in Central Europe, the Soviet Union, and the Middle East.

Dr. Ward is associate professor of journalism at Temple University in Philadelphia, Pennsylvania.

He and his wife make their home in Warrington, Pennsylvania.